PENGUIN BOOKS

BLACK JOY

BLACK JOY

JOY

Edited by
**Charlie Brinkhurst-Cuff
& Timi Sotire**

PENGUIN BOOKS

PENGUIN BOOKS

UK | USA | Canada | Ireland | Australia
India | New Zealand | South Africa

Penguin Books is part of the Penguin Random House group of companies
whose addresses can be found at global.penguinrandomhouse.com.

www.penguin.co.uk   www.puffin.co.uk   www.ladybird.co.uk

Penguin
Random House
UK

First published 2021

001

Text copyright © Diane Abbott, Faridah Àbíké-Íyímídé, Fopé Ajanaku, Athian Akec,
Travis Alabanza, Haaniyah Angus, Rukiat Ashawe, Bukky Bakray, Richie Brave,
Munya Chawawa, Ruby Fatimilehin, Theophina Gabriel, Lauryn Green, Ife Grillo,
Isaac James, Chanté Joseph, Vanessa Kisuule, Henrie Kwushue, Tobi Kyeremateng,
Mikai McDermott, Jason Okundaye, Tope Olufemi, Melz Owusu, Leigh-Anne Pinnock,
Mayowa Quadri, Timi Sotire, Lavinya Stennett, Sophia Tassew, 2021

Illustrations copyright © Jovilee Burton (page 117), Tomekah George (pages 158 and 369)
Emma Hall (pages 24 and 247), Chioma Ince (pages 73 and 324),
Olivia Twist (page 199), 2021

The moral right of the authors and illustrators has been asserted

Typeset in Sabon LT Std
Text design by Mandy Norman
Printed and bound in Great Britain by Clays Ltd, Elcograf S.p.A.

The authorized representative in the EEA is Penguin Random House Ireland, Morrison
Chambers, 32 Nassau Street, Dublin D02 YH68

A CIP catalogue record for this book is available from the British Library

ISBN: 978-0-241-51966-0

All correspondence to:
Penguin Books, Penguin Random House Children's
One Embassy Gardens, 8 Viaduct Gardens, London SW11 7BW

To anyone struggling, or who has struggled
to find joy.

C. B. C.

To my friends and family,
for their constant and unwavering support.

T. S.

Contents

The essays contained in this book cover a wide range of topics and themes and we'd like to advise readers that some of the content could therefore be upsetting. Where possible we have flagged specific essays for potentially triggering content.

Foreword

Charlie Brinkhurst-Cuff

JOURNALIST, BOOK EDITOR, COLUMNIST & PODCAST HOST

Black joy is the infectious laughter of my mum and aunty. It is my dad telling me to be proud of my heritage. It is the feeling of hopping along to my first 'Candy' dance. It is stepping off the plane in Jamaica. It is the heart surge of hearing a chant that resonates with me at a protest. The smooth stretch and pull of my afro acquiescing its curl to a box braid. It is a look of recognition. It is shared and it is individual. It is all of these things and more.

Black joy is essential but difficult to define. It means different things to different people, and you'd be right to question whether it is simply any joy experienced by a Black person at any time or something beyond that. But this book, featuring the essays of twenty-eight Black British minds, tries to make the links between individual joy and the collective experience. As unique people and as a wide-ranging community, we embody and have created space for such profound moments of joy that there would never be enough pages to capture them all. But we've tried!

The essays within *Black Joy* speak of many things I already knew to bring the Black British community joy, from the big boldness of Carnival to the low hum of the clippers in the barbershop. They also touch on many things I was less aware of. Until I read Travis Alabanza's essay on Prince, I shamefully knew next to nothing about the 1980s popstar whose iconic status has uplifted the hearts of the Black gender-nonconforming community now flourishing in his wake. Before Rukiat Ashawe bared her soul by talking about her journey with existential nihilism against the backdrop of an identity she was told would always go hand in hand with hardship, I didn't fully comprehend that believing nothing really matters could lead to joy.

We cannot completely get away from the fact that everyone's life is spliced with some amount of pain – without a spectrum of emotions, of course, we wouldn't feel joy in quite the same way. As I write this, George Floyd's murderer, Derek Chauvin, has just received a sentence that will see him jailed for many years, while yet another family grieves the loss of their daughter, sixteen-year-old Ma'Khia Bryant. In the UK, we are marking the anniversary of the death of Stephen Lawrence. These essays are uplifting, but they do not ignore the raw realities of our existence – and nor should they. Black joy in this climate is an undoubtedly political reaction to the climate we are living in, but we must be careful to push the conversation beyond this moment, and beyond a hashtag.

'Joy is a way to enter the pain as much as it is to be in the joy,' Kleaver Cruz, the Dominican–American founder of The Black Joy Project, tells me. With his own book launching in 2022, he has interviewed over a thousand people across the African diaspora on what Black joy means to them and he continues to cite Black joy as a form of resistance and resilience. 'There's a difference between experiencing something and creating it,' he goes on. 'When you consciously create Black joy or conjure it, it becomes something you can wield as opposed to just experience.'

I don't believe there is yet a substantial body of work on Black joy in the same way there is about Black trauma, even though they often exist in tandem. But soon come. In March 2021, the actor and producer Marsai Martin spoke out about her 'no Black pain' rule, saying she doesn't want to produce projects that centre on Black trauma because there are enough of them already out there. It's essential we move towards storytelling that allows for a full spectrum of emotion. As put by my co-editor, the brilliant new talent that is Timi Sotire: 'Re-imagining what it means to be Black by focusing on what makes our community happy is paramount at a time like this.' I hope this book becomes part of a joyous canon.

It can feel indulgent to focus on the things that make your heart sing, on the golden moments of light and laughter. We're often made to feel like we must be deserving of joy, that to lean in to the emotion first we need to have suffered. Or that our suffering is so great that joy is incomprehensible. Or that we have done too many 'bad' things to be gifted with joy. I want this book to challenge that notion. Especially if you are a Black person, you deserve joy regardless of the life you've lived. Joy doesn't have to be contingent upon anything but existence. This book should leave you with the knowledge cemented that Black joy is multiplicious – a bursting from the seams of experiences and inner mantras.

It is also by and for a young Black British audience. It is unashamedly FUBU, because we deserve it. We deserve our own slice of heaven, a big tiered cake of goodness as we continue to navigate the rocky waters of youth. To our Black readers, your joy is so valid, so important to be shared, to be found and exposed.

The infrastructure for Black joy in Britain is still being built. We do have a road to travel, one that needs signposts along the way. But I've never been surer that this book, on Black British joy specifically, needs to exist and that it will help in the construction. It is one web of interconnected stories that will hopefully create glistening threads leading readers directly to their own joy. Especially if you are a Black person, you deserve joy in all its many facets and intricacies. Black joy can be your love, your light and your fight.

Kleaver puts it perfectly: 'The work that's happening is giving language to what we know to be real in the world. It's part of survival. Joy is innate, it's not a racial thing. But there's just something particular when we're doing it . . . Blackness is infinite. In all the ways we show up, that's how many ways Black joy can show up or be defined.'

Our Blackness is a construct, but that doesn't mean the ways in which we can find happiness within it are any less profound.

To you, with joy in my heart,

Charlie Brinkhurst-Cuff

X

Foreword

Timi Sotire
JOURNALIST & EDITOR

For most of my life, I've associated my Blackness with endurance. I've endured racism; I've endured trauma. When growing up in a world structured by race, and anchored by white supremacy, it's hard not to feel this way. I'm proud of being Black because, in spite of the struggle, I've managed to find moments of joy in my life. I love my Blackness, but it's always been hard for me to conceptualize it outside the lens of Black trauma. And it's not like society has encouraged me to do otherwise! British society is designed to remind Black people of their second-class status, from the news we read to the TV we watch. Even most of the Black community's success stories are underpinned by the idea of fighting through the pain and coming out on top. Although these stories are inspiring, if this is all you see growing up, it inevitably takes a toll on you. In my early twenties, I found that I'd created a mental trap for myself where I'd feel guilty if I experienced joy without having to fight for it. Do you know how exhausting that is?

While working on *Black Joy*, I've been forced to think about my Blackness in a different way. I've learned that joy and other healthy emotions require an element of intentionality. We have to choose to feel love, joy and care – they need to be sought out and become a practice in one's life. I've come to realize that I don't need to feel joy *despite* the hardship; sometimes I can just be happy, and that is OK! Choosing to feel this way, and freeing myself from the guilt that I've long associated with my joy, has been liberating. I've made a choice to reaffirm this sentiment, every day, for the rest of my life.

I've given five new writers the space to discuss what brings them joy. Tope has written an evocative account of why barbershops are a safe space for Black people who get trims; Mikai's done a great job in outlining how Black beauty is radical and community-building. Theophina's story will make you hungry: she's written the most beautiful essay on souse and how it brings generations of families together. Haaniyah, my favourite film critic, has written about the UK film industry and what needs to be done in order to centre Black joy on-screen. Last but not least, Fopé's essay on Black love is pure poetry and made me cry on the first read.

One reason why I love these essays, and all the essays in the anthology, is that they provide a real insight into the minds of members of our community. *Black Joy* isn't a prescriptive body of work; we aren't telling Black Brits what *should* make them happy. It's impossible for us to capture all facets of Black joy, but we hope that our Black readers find parts of themselves in these essays. For the Black readers who haven't grown up within their racial communities, this is also for you. It's easy to feel like your upbringing has ostracized you to the point where you merely exist on the periphery of Blackness. But my own essay on discovering joy among strangers should act as a reminder that Black joy can be found in the absence of a physical Black community.

To our Black readers, I want you to remember that our joy should be at the core of our being. Our joy isn't something that needs to be explained or justified; it's our God-given right! When we find the things that bring us joy, whether it's hanging out with our friends, watching anime or listening to music, we shouldn't let that joy go. We should do our best to keep it. Forever.

Timi Sotire

BLACK JOY

Life is Just a Party

Prince and my revolution

Travis Alabanza

PERFORMANCE ARTIST,
WRITER, & THEATRE-MAKER

OK, I hate to be one of those writers who set homework before we've even finished the text together, but today I am going to do exactly that. Class, please put down your reading glasses, shut this book and head to the visiting lecturer for today's lesson: YouTube. Once there, make yourself comfortable and find the video for 'Kiss' by Prince and The Revolution. Click on to full-screen mode once you have found it. In fact, if you have a projector, put it on the projector. Or, better than that, grab someone else's laptop so you can watch it on two screens side by side. Go ahead and put the sound on as loud as you can without your flatmate/mother/neighbour causing a fuss. Basically, do whatever is in your power to make sure the next three minutes and fifty-six seconds are all about this video.

Ready?

Press play, and then come back to this book when you are done.

Three minutes and fifty-six seconds pass.

A few more extra seconds for those who didn't bookmark this page and spent some time trying to find where they were.

OK, now at least we are on the same page.

If you're like me then you'll have watched that video for the 972nd time in your life, and each time you'll still be blown away by it. You'll know every beat, every jolt of the neck, every moment he gazes straight into the camera. You'll be able to recall when you watched it for the first time fourteen years ago as a confused young Black-mixed kid (who at this point had only stolen their mother's lipstick once) and felt a confusing mix of love, adoration, desire and empowerment. When you watched it for the first time, you'll have sat staring at the blank screen. Maybe you'll have rubbed your eyes to check that what you watched was real, looked around the room to make sure no one else had seen your bewilderment. And so you'll have pressed replay, ready to watch and watch and watch until it was someone else's turn to use the internet (this was 2007 and not everyone had broadband or access to YouTube then). You'll have sat there taking notes, staring at all the details, wondering why no one had ever told you about Prince and this music video before. You'll have been in an ecstasy of emotion and felt personally betrayed that this was not obligatory viewing to qualify as a citizen of this world.

At fourteen, I did not have the language to describe what was happening to me at that moment. But now, over ten years later, I can name it with as much clarity and strength as one of

Prince's thrusts: watching this video was the beginning of my revolution.

REVOLUTION (noun)**:**
a forcible overthrow of a current order, in favour
of a new system

Calling this video the beginning of my revolution may sound like a grand statement, but when you are fourteen every change within you feels momentous. I mean that not in a negative or patronizing way but in a way I wish I still felt. The older you get, the more change feels like a chore. In my adolescence, change felt like explosions bursting through my skin, like my body being taken over with impulse or being caught in the rain, yet continuing to dance anyway. In my teens, the action associated with change often came well before any rumination on what the consequences would be. I was led by instinct and motion. Now it comes with overthinking, meticulous planning and far too many coloured highlighters to ever feel as powerful as a revolution. I long for the change of my teen years.

If a revolution is an overthrow of a previous order, then to understand the ways this video kickstarted a revolution for me, you have to be aware of the order and the regime I had been working within. I was a new fourteen, meaning that puberty was well settled into my body but the confidence to defy it, which often comes near the latter end of the teens, wasn't within me yet. I was in that stage where hair was growing, my voice was changing and my moods swinging, but at a pace that meant I was yet to be in control of it.

Puberty felt like it was always seven steps ahead of me. I was awkward. Not awkward enough that people would use that word to describe me, but I felt it in every crevice of my body. I had spent much of my time as a thirteen-year-old realizing that, due to my effeminate gestures, desire for more out-there clothing and what other people saw as a queer identity (which I was still unaware of), I would have more attention drawn towards me than others. It was not always positive. My next year was not spent changing my appearance or hiding, but I carried around a tiredness that I do not think is natural to have when you are so young. A tiredness that was caused by constantly having to dodge or manage people's reactions to my authenticity.

Choosing to be anyone but myself was not an option – that hurt far too much – but I soon realized that choosing to be myself (that is, to be gender nonconforming) was to go hand in hand with feeling disempowered, undesirable and weak. Wearing eyeshadow for the first time became associated with boys laughing at me at the corner shop of my estate. Trying on a women's jumper in the New Look store in town triggered a group of teens calling me a homophobic slur. Every instance of transgressing gender, trying to push beyond the barriers of what was prescribed for a kid that looked like me, was punished by the outside world. That was just the way things were. That was the order I was working within.

*'I just want your extra time and your
Kiss'*

Prince seemed to exist in a world that felt free, or at least unfazed by punishment. In Prince's order, the danger of gender nonconformity was forgotten and replaced with the pure seduction of his talent. As I stared into the eyes of my new order, those of Prince and The Revolution, my past felt unimportant. My eyes became binoculars, zooming into every pixel of the video, spotting the eyeliner flicking from Prince's eyes, the hem of his crop top showing off his sculpted stomach, his hands moving with the flourishes that I was punished for in my previous order. I watched as he danced with an abundance of colour and energy without anyone holding him back.

I had so many questions about this man. Was he even a man? Was he still alive? Did he have friends? But they all became irrelevant as the track picked up and my bedroom became the concert I had snuck out of my house to attend.

I grabbed the crop top I had been hiding under my bed and waved it in the air as if it belonged to Prince himself. I danced and spun in the bliss of seeing someone who could be close to sharing the energy I had. Without knowing any of the words, I sang to Prince as if we had shared the same songbook, brimming with the ecstasy of seeing someone else changing rules I had thought were immovable.

As soon as I finished watching the video on a loop for an hour, I started my further reading, which included watching compilation videos of Prince's most iconic fashion moments (including those assless chaps), as well as every music video I could find. Yet I would always end the Prince binge by watching the 'Kiss' video one last time.

I had never seen a person like Prince before. Someone who had my skin tone, who the world was calling a man, who seemed to defy what it meant to hold on to such rigid masculinity. But more than what I was seeing, it was what I could tell that Prince was feeling: Confidence. Power. Desire. Celebration. His head did not hang low in his difference; it was higher than anyone else's in the room.

Compared to what can feel like the rigid gender policing of the 2020s, Prince existed in what I see as a far more gender anarchic and fluid period of the 1980s. Boy George and Annie Lennox had built on the smudged lines of gender that David Bowie had drawn, yet none of them held a hair texture or skin

" I could tell what Prince was feeling: **Confidence. Power. Desire. Celebration.** His head did not hang low in his difference; it was higher than anyone else's in the room " tone like mine – no matter how many perms they applied. Prince was different. His androgyny cut through different racial communities, his brown skin adorned in a trademark purple as he shot magazine cover after magazine cover in stockings, blazers, crop tops – and always with a healthy swish of eyeliner.

In Prince's early career moments, many critics found his defiance of boxes a frustration, often critiquing and insulting him because they could not understand him. Yet Prince did not hide. In fact, he began to speak to the critics directly, with lines such as 'I'm not a woman, I'm not a man/ I am something that you'll never understand' feeling like a personal retaliation. By the time of his hit 'Purple Rain', Prince was lauded by rebels and straight-edged mums alike, and in naming his backing band The Revolution it felt like Prince was talking directly to us: you either take on board the change, or this order is not for you.

In my previous order, all I could associate transgression with was loss. I was only fourteen yet already trying to decide whether changing who I was and not being my authentic self would be the choice that would bring me the most joy. Seeing how negatively people responded to my breaking of gender norms made me feel like that was the only reality I would ever exist within, and that I could not experience anything different. Yet here, transported into Prince's music video and learning about his life, I saw someone who was being celebrated for all the things I had come to believe would bring the opposite. Someone who pushed past initial judgement to prove others wrong. Someone who showed me that being gender nonconforming and Black did not have to go hand in hand with hiding or hurt.

Throughout Prince's career, he was commended for his fashion choices and his ability to break down barriers with alluring confidence. When he died, countless people flooded the streets in purple to celebrate his influence. Prince's authenticity and passion inspired so many waves of future Black artists. Janelle Monáe's *Rolling Stone* interview in which she comes out to the world as queer is littered with references and allusions to Prince. And in an interview with BBC Radio 1's Annie Mac, she said: 'Prince growing up was always otherworldly to me, to the point where I was almost scared of him. When I would see his videos on TV they would make me very scared, mainly because I had never seen a Black man express himself in the way that Prince did.' And it is this that strikes me: how much people's initial fear of Prince's difference turned into an appreciation and joy. People did not love him *despite* his differences, but because of them. The way that his transgression of expectation, of what a Black person is positioned to be, of what masculinity and femininity could

" I remember the revolution that is possible in **choosing myself"**

look like – ultimately Prince's authenticity – could not just spark joy in himself, but in others around him went against everything I knew to be possible.

I do not think revolutions should feel easy and this one definitely didn't. Revolutions take time to move past doubt and resistance and ultimately create change on the other side. I think of how boycotts in my home town of Bristol had to happen for Black people to be able to work on buses. Or how bricks had to be thrown and people arrested for LGBTQIA+ lives to progress and improve. Prince pushed past resistance, and as I started looking at him I could see I would have to as well. I felt resistance. It felt confusing, contradictory and untrue. I remember at first searching for evidence that Prince was not in fact beloved by many, scanning the internet for hate articles that ridiculed him for his outfits and expression. But the more I searched, the more I not only fell in love but learned of generations of love for him too. It was in that learning, when I moved away from denial, that I moved into the joy of possibility. If aunties and uncles could love him, then maybe, in turn, they could love me? Or more importantly, whether or not they loved me, from Prince's existence came the reality that I was deserving of love and joy and celebration and should go where I could find it.

That was the revolutionary change happening through watching the video: the realization that gender-nonconformity could and should bring joy; that transgression of expectations could and should be met with laughter and smiles and celebration. Watching and dancing to Prince did not change the realities of what was said towards me and those who acted or looked like me on the streets, in the classrooms or in the church. I did not end the video and suddenly step into a world where I had adoring fans, boys throwing themselves over me or eyes staring only lovingly. This was not an external revolution. Rather, dancing to Prince and looking at him own every part of any room he was in created an internal shift about what is and could be possible for me. It was a grounding point to go back to.

After I wore a dress outside for the first time and saw the whole council estate I lived on fill with stares, I could run back to my room and blast Prince, losing myself in the new order that reminded me there are other emotions to feel within gender-nonconformity. Later on in my life, when I received my first rejection from a boy because I was wearing make-up, I could escape to the video of Prince and see him exude desirability and confidence that reminded me that it was possible. Ultimately, when the external world created uncontrollable scenarios, finding joy in the charisma and power of someone else became a lifeline, a motivation and a possibility. Prince reminds us that situations can change, that we are rewarded for authenticity and that there is something revolutionary in defying expectations.

Three minutes and fifty-six seconds pass again, as I watch the video one last time for the day. And I remember the revolution that is possible in choosing myself.

FIND YOUR OWN JOY

Put on an outfit you've always been afraid to wear and blast 'Kiss' by Prince in your room as if it's your own sold-out concert.

Welcome to the Masquerade
How Carnival makes space for everyone

Isaac James

WRITER, LAWYER & CO-FOUNDER
OF THE BLACK MEN IN LAW NETWORK

Illustration by Emma Hall

I am the Masquerade, and the Masquerade is in me.

I am a man with grandparents born in four different locations on the island that straddles the meeting point of the tranquil Caribbean Sea and the turbulent Atlantic Ocean: Dominica, *the nature isle*. Boetica, Délices, Canefield and Pointe Michel – all four are part of me and in some way I am part of them. They are the four elements of my being: earth, air, fire and water, all converging harmoniously into this one body. It may not seem apparent at this stage in the story, but I will need them all to make my way through the Masquerade or 'Mas'.

I myself grew up in Bradford in West Yorkshire, surrounded by the peers of my grandparents born in Dominica and other Caribbean islands, many of whom journeyed to Britain together in the 1950s and early 1960s. To those of us second- and third-generation Caribbean Brits, the Carnival season is everything. Past and present, we have made our presence known with Carnival celebrations from Luton to Leeds, and from Cardiff to Coventry. The biggest of these is Notting Hill, which began in 1959 as the indoor Carnival spearheaded by Trinidadian journalist Claudia Jones. Over time it has blossomed into the biggest Caribbean Carnival outside of the Caribbean itself, with over two million attendees each year. Carnival becomes the hub of the local mixing with the national blending with the international.

There is no better time of year than Carnival. The Carnival season, which takes place in the few days preceding Lent in the Caribbean (but throughout the summer months in the UK), is a joyous but also highly emotional one.

Carnival is the one time in which all of the cadences and flows of the music rock your body and you can simply let loose. Everyone is on show. It doesn't matter if you are fat, thin, tall, short, of darker or lighter complexion, whether you are disabled or non-disabled – Mas is for *everybody*. During the pre-Mas fetes and J'Ouvert events (the daybreak tradition of Carnival), we fling paint, powder and water at each other gladly: *yuh cya play Mas if yuh fraid powder*. This is a preternatural, spiritual and ancestral experience only comparable to the highest forms of human pleasure. The essence of the siwo (the effervescent Kwéyòl term for Carnival) is captured in the concentrated frown of your brother, the longing eyes of your sister, the flailing limbs of your lover and the closeness of our bodies as we embrace one another for the whine – deep, fast, slow and tender. This is serious business.

Since the beginning of time, African peoples have been at the forefront of great discoveries and creations. Pliny the Elder, the Roman natural philosopher, even commented that 'semper aliquid novi Africam adferre' – Africa *always* brings something new. Now, over six thousand kilometres away from their old home, the descendants of the Yoruba, Fante, Wolof, Mandé, Fula and Mandinka continue the great tradition of kwèyé hòd anyen, creating out of nothing. Each time I gather with my people to continue this four-hundred-year-old tradition, we make it anew.

Who would have thought that one of the gravest genocides the world has ever seen, the transatlantic slave trade, where over ten million Africans were kidnapped and trafficked into slavery in the Americas from the sixteenth to the nineteenth century, would generate such an ardent culture, burning bright with the fires of resistance? Despite the multiple attempts by European colonial powers to crush the West African heart within the Caribbean, it kept beating. People from the smallest part of the world, in some of its least populated islands, created a culture that transformed the way in which we view moving celebrations.

I think about the way that Carnival is just simply Carnival to my grandmother. She grew up in Canefield, Dominica, in the 1930s and 1940s, and she first experienced Carnival as a little girl. To her, it was just a loud rabble and she couldn't stand the noise. In some ways, this makes sense: J'Ouvert is *loud*. In order to signify the arrival of the season, horns are blown, whistles scream, and in places such as Grenada the clattering heels of the djab-djab make their presence known. The Carnival 'devils', rendered in the darkest tar or paint to represent our ancestors, would move a sleepy village into action. The small bands move from the countryside villages towards town, and as they get closer they get louder and louder and louder. For my grandmother, even to this day, Carnival is just an event that occurs annually. But to me? Carnival is the tie that binds me to centuries of history and it means the world. I can be my fullest, truest Caribbean self within it, and the winds of the Ramajay (the Trini term for going on bad and creatively dancing) carry me through the season. I feel rooted, like I'm a branch on a wide tree of my heritage, like my father and his father before him.

Carnival is a culture that belongs in the hands of the rebels, the downtrodden and those at the bottom of the pigmentocracy. The most predominant form of Carnival – or, as those of us close to the culture know it, Mas – began in the French Caribbean colonial territories of Guadeloupe, Dominica, St Lucia, Martinique and Grenada. The colourful masquerade balls and dances were a strong feature of the French ruling class of plantation owners who enslaved Black people throughout the Antilles in the eighteenth century. The Carnival season ends in an explosive manner, with a series of marker points along the way. From Samedi Gras to J'Ouvert to Mardi Gras, when the French estate-owning classes visited each other they held great Creole fetes. Meanwhile, in a colourful and very West African fashion, our ancestors

" Carnival is the tie that binds me to centuries of history and it means the world. **I can be my fullest, truest Caribbean self within it** " danced outside, imitating those who enslaved them, and enjoyed the few moments of respite they were able to receive under the blistering heat of the sun. When we do the same thing in the twenty-first century I feel such pride. Who would have thought that we'd continue to honour our ancestors' traditions from the 1600s? No matter how hard they try, they can't hold us down.

I think about my childhood and how attending Leeds Carnival was a special trip. Contrary to my behaviour now as a diehard feter, I did not attend Carnival frequently as a child because of a family curse. While attending a Leeds Carnival outing with the Dominican community in the 1970s, my paternal grandmother was hit by a bottle and injured. The community she travelled with were aware of who caused the harm. In turn, the August bank holiday weekend became one of mixed emotion. In an interesting way, my father unwittingly continued the tradition of remembering the pain of one of his forebears, much like we do at Mas on a wider scale. In typical stoic Caribbean-father style, he stubbornly refused to let us attend Carnival and only divulged the true reason to my mother. As with many emotional tales affecting Caribbean men, my brother and I only discovered this by chance once my mother grew tired of us missing Leeds Carnival, which she had attended many times as a young girl.

On the few occasions when I did attend Leeds Carnival, I

remember my mother holding me close as my eyes widened in surprise at seeing people with skin tones just like mine celebrating the Vaval in fiery and electric ways, gyrating their waists in such a *strange* but rhythmic manner. I remember being around nine years old and asking my mother, 'Mum, what's *that* that they're doing? That hip thing?' She laughed. 'Welcome to the culture, little one,' she replied. 'This is *whining*. It's a dance and it's how *we* dance.'

I longed to be one of the lucky children masquerading down the road on Children's Day, which took place on Sunday and was the only day I could attend. I also wanted to go on the Monday, but my mother said that was a no-go. I didn't understand why until I was about twenty-four and I first attended Carnival as an adult . . . and, well, then I understood completely. Carnival Monday is *wild*. Carnival Monday for us in the UK is Carnival Tuesday for people in the Caribbean. It is the fulcrum of the Carnival experience. It's the day of Pretty Mas, when everybody dresses in their finery and the exquisite skill of Carnival costume designers is finally revealed. Every detail is on show, and if you are a masquerader your costume is the ticket to the hottest festivities of the year. The night before is the most exciting and spine-tingling. I always feel slightly nervous – I'm going to be on *show*. When I don my costume for Pretty Mas, I am transformed. I quite simply look and feel *divine* and everybody knows it.

Emma Hall

*

Carnival as we know it in the UK is hundreds of years old. It was born out of the convergence of three movements of empire: the Spanish, the French and the British, after all three had colonized various Caribbean islands and enslaved Africans for centuries. It is modelled on Trinidad Carnival, which came about after King Carlos III of Spain approved the Cédula de Población in 1783, a law that allowed immigration into Trinidad from neighbouring French Caribbean islands, giving slave owners tax breaks.

Within a decade of the approval of the Cédula, Trinidad's population had boomed to over 18,000 residents compared to a few thousand only a decade before. French planters, along with those they enslaved, and free people of colour all flooded into Trinidad, and this is where the magic began. The enslaved from different islands mixed with the enslaved in Trinidad, and a beautiful, much larger culture was born. What we know as Carnival culture can be found today across the Caribbean on various islands. After all, we all have the same ancestors. It is this mixture of Caribbean people that we see replicated in Carnivals up and down the United Kingdom. As Caribbean people, we are always migrating and creating hubs and networks wherever we settle.

We continue the same traditions in the UK as we *chip down di road* with our call and response to the soca songs, the prosody of which perfectly match the riddim and the lyrics, replicating the chanté Mas while proudly singing the lavwé chorus. Like our ancestors of old in the Caribbean, we are the matadors, the djamettes, the red ochres, the bad-johns and the sensay who meet the djab molassie, the lansé kòd, the djab djab and the nèg gwo siwo that stain the roads black with tar and paint, donning chains that represent the cords used to bind their ancestors, along with horns to appear even more frightening. The anger of our forebears is alive and well. As we pass down each road, we flirt with history, reality and fantasy. From time to time, a moko jumbie passes, twice as tall as the tallest man, conquering the air as they wade through it on 15-foot-high stilts in their elaborate satin costume, dancing to the beat of the music. They make the impossible possible.

As we head to the streets, I am reminded of how, after being emancipated from slavery, the freed people brought the Masquerade to the streets from the estate. I think of how in Dominica in the eighteenth and nineteenth centuries, especially in the towns of Portsmouth and Roseau, the labourers, fishermen and domestic workers were joined by the bands from the villages across the island to destroy the lofty behavioural standards of the ruling class. They would become loud, unrespectable and effectively uncontrollable people. The ruling class, also participating in Mas, did the reverse, performing as characters such as the nèg jaden, the field slave. People would take the opportunity to reverse societal status for a day, showing us that, in a way, class and identity are human fabrications.

There are still those who seek to reproduce patterns of harm by bringing patriarchal terms and conditions to the Val. There are times in certain bands and spaces where people feel entitled to women and objectify them, or dominate over queer and trans people. It is common to hear of people speak on social media of how they have felt uncomfortable after experiencing violence at the hands of men when attending Carnival, and these traumatizing experiences make people not want to attend in the future. But what I love most about Carnival is that there is great power and liberation within it. Women create safety units to whine and to enjoy being together. There is no trouble, simply enjoyment. Queer and trans people build whining circles where we let freedom reign. There is no performance of compulsory heterosexuality – we just enjoy being. It is this part of Carnival that people do not understand. It is a space where you can just be free. Everyone, irrespective of body size or shape, is welcome.

Our ancestors created spaces for us to truly be whoever we wanted to be. In Carnival, there was traditionally cross-gender expression, inversion of gender norms and mockery of the slave-owning classes, with characters such as Dame

Lorraine, a parody of the French colonial aristocratic wife, with her padded posterior and breasts and floral print dress, played by men. So too was the character of Baby Doll, a gaily dressed woman with a frilled dress and bonnet who carries a doll to symbolize an illegitimate baby and stops male passers-by to accuse them of being the father and demand money to buy milk. Upon emancipation, our ancestors took the term literally and metaphorically to see beyond the restrictive lens of gender, and I truly love it.

Carnival represents the ever-expansive potential of African creativity even under the worst circumstances. They say it takes extreme pressure to create a diamond; Carnival culture is one created out of the most extreme stresses any human could ever endure, and at Carnival there are millions of diamonds shining bright. This is the one time where we can forget about the pain we endure. From sunrise, we are bards turning stories into a beautiful chorus, harmonizing in unison. I feel at peace with my friends and those who respect the culture.

It is at the closing of the day, when I am on my way home at sunset, that I am reminded that this is the greatest show on earth . . . and I'm damn proud.

FIND YOUR OWN JOY

We honour those who came before us by remembering the music of old. Listen to some zouk, calypso, soca and kadans-lypso from the 1970s and 1980s and free up yuhself!

Black Banter
The importance of having a work BFF

Munya Chawawa

SATIRIST

The workplace. For many, it's a slightly stuffy office with a jammed printer, the fragrant cocktail of BO and Febreeze, and a cheese plant . . . slowly dying in the corner . . . because Huw from finance keeps pouring his dutty coffee on to it. However, if you're Black, the workplace is also a minefield of microaggressions. It's a never-ending barrage of questions by people whose cultural knowledge peaks at knowing the chorus to 'Hakuna Matata'. It's the endless interrogation over what Stormzy *actually* meant in his latest single – as if you both sat together in his kitchen hashing out the lyrics over some pounded yam and prosecco. It's constantly combatting your co-workers' curiosity: no, Sue, we don't put cocoa butter on toast; yes, Steve, we generally tend to tan when the temperature is over 40 degrees Celsius; and no, Cheryl, there are no Airbnbs in Wakanda, so maybe stick to Cornwall this summer. To put it succinctly, being Black in the workplace can be exhausting.

In some ways, it's harmless. People ask questions because they're intrigued or perhaps uninformed and they trust you enough to approach you for an answer. To a degree, we might even be the bridge between ignorance and education. Poor Gareth could be one sip of Stella away from joining the EDL and you might just be his melanin messiah, my friend! Surely it doesn't hurt to spare a moment or two bringing people you work with up to speed on a race or culture they know next to nothing about? No one's asking you to get up on stage, dressed in a black beret, and start reeling off a medley of Nelson Mandela's greatest hits. It's literally just a five-minute chat about something you know better than anyone, right? Perhaps. But it's a little tricky getting your Malcolm X on when you've got a sixty-page assignment, an online first-aid course and a performance review – all before you've even had one sad mouthful of your Pret porridge. We got things to do! Black people don't sit around at work waiting to deliver TED Talks to people actually called Ted. We find work as tedious and testing as anyone does – the deadlines, the daily meetings, the death-stares you get for not chipping in for a Colin the Caterpillar cake for the receptionist who literally calls a SWAT team every time you sign in. We dislike it just as much as anyone. Which is why asking us to be employees *and* shining beacons of BAME illumination is sometimes a bit too much to bear.

It's been a while since I wrote an essay, but if I remember one thing from my GCSEs it's point-evidence-explain. Oh, and also the bleak ending to *Of Mice and Men* (if you know, you know). Anyway, I feel like I've made a point and explained it – but where's my evidence? Where are the cold hard facts? Well, our story begins in 2008 . . .

Just to be clear, I wasn't born in 2008 – because if I was, I wouldn't be writing this. I'd probably be filming a TikTok where I'm grinding against my wardrobe to a Megan Thee Stallion song. Actually, 2008 is when I got my first job. With the help of my mum, I managed to land a gig working in a very posh restaurant, even though the height of my culinary experience was burning a carrot in food tech. By the way, when I say posh, I mean *posh*. This was the type of place where you'd get fired if there wasn't enough gold leaf sprinkled on a customer's dessert. Put it this way: if it hadn't been for my mum (a white lady, who worked for the owner of the village the restaurant was in), I don't think I would have got the job.

Things started off innocently enough, but my colleagues just couldn't seem to get my name right. Between my bosses and the other waiting staff, I went from being Manuel to Man-U, Manyé to Munda, and, my personal favourite, William. And yet these same colleagues were strutting over to customers and offering them the option of foie gras or boeuf bourguignon with perfect French pronunciation. It was then I began to wonder: were they saying my name wrong because they *couldn't* get it right or because they *didn't care* about getting it right?

A few months and several smashed champagne flutes later, I was quite enjoying the life of a silver-service waiter. By this point, I'd made good friends with the rest of the team, and just about convinced a hobbit-like pot-washer to stop calling me 'nig-nog'. Turns out he loved a cheeky beer between wash cycles, so I'd sneak behind the bar when it got really busy and smuggle him a couple of Budweiser's finest *non-alcoholic* beers. He never once found out about this beer-based bamboozling. Clearly, it's quite tricky telling the difference when you're busy being a racist. Anyhow, by this point I basically had the staff onside, but now it was the customers who were proving a little tricky.

We had been called out to cater at the Royal Norfolk Show, which was essentially Wireless for farmers. However, instead of Cardi B or Burna Boy headlining the main stage, there would be a man walking an unusually large cow around in circles while people clapped politely. The real action took place in the catering tent – a ginormous marquee filled with white-clothed tables and hundreds of shimmering trays of expensive champagne. It was here that the richest of the rich stopped by for a quick bite before going off to admire a selection of tractors. We had to be on our best behaviour: no mistakes, no messing up and, most importantly, no forgetting that the customer is *always* right. We were about six hours into the shift when we hit the lunchtime rush – hundreds of affluent aristocrats bumbled into the tent with their elaborate hats and flushed faces. For the next two hours, we worked like clockwork, the perfect fusion of efficiency and charm as we dished out dauphinoise potatoes and roast duck at breakneck speed. The camaraderie was real. Even though not a word passed between us, we synchronized like Olympic swimmers, dodging and ducking between dishes, occasionally managing to fire off a cheeky grin that said, 'We're smashing this, innit?!' And then there was the incident.

I had been put on potato duty, which meant that after all the meals had been served I had to go round with a gigantic tray of potatoes, because, you know, being filthy rich requires a lot of carbs. However, as you can imagine, when it's over 30 degrees Celsius outside and you're stood in a massive plastic tent balancing boiling potatoes, one does tend to sweat. As I shimmied my way between two rather large men, who were bellowing about some hilarious mishap in the cricket changing rooms, one of them turned and saw me struggling with the tray, beads of sweat rolling off my forehead. He reached up and plucked a potato off the pile like it was a big beige grape. And before he turned away, he looked at me dead in the eye and said, 'I bet you're used to this heat, aren't you, boy?'

It took a few minutes to process what he meant, but I understood eventually. He was implying that because I was brown, I must have come from Africa, where it was hot. To this sweaty Sherlock Holmes, there was no plausible way that I, a brown boy, could have been born here in England. As I headed back to the kitchen, I caught two of the other waiters on their way out and told them what had happened. They both laughed . . . and so I began laughing too. As the story got round, the laughter spread through the kitchen as I recalled the incident with more and more vigour each time. My anecdote seemed to be the highlight of a deliriously busy day, and as good as it felt to be sat there in the kitchen laughing with everyone, some part of me felt like I wasn't laughing because it was funny – I was laughing because I didn't have a choice.

I left the restaurant after a few years – not because of the race stuff, but because I wanted to branch out from potatoes to other root vegetables. However, the Royal Norfolk Show seemed to be the start of a string of similar experiences. Things like customers complimenting me on how good my English was, or being the only person given the day off when we catered for the Queen once. (To be fair, I probably dodged a bullet by not working that day – literally. There were snipers on the cathedral, and I don't think they would have taken too kindly to a brown waiter approaching Her Majesty with a carving knife.) After leaving, I worked in a few other places where people would get my name wrong or make jokes that felt a bit UKIP-y, but I kept my head down and continued grinding for that minimum wage (not in a TikTok kind of way). Eventually, I ended up working for a music channel and it was there that I met my first Black co-worker.

I worked at the channel for a couple of years and made some good friends, but the week after I moved to London to be closer to the job I was made redundant. Fortunately, it didn't last too long, and by sticking to a diet that solely consisted of pasta and baked beans (together) I kept afloat until they rehired me. On my first day back, I bounced into the office, greeting familiar faces on the way to my beloved desk, where I plonked myself down on to a pin that my friend Will had left as a 'welcome back' present. But something was different. A new team had joined and was sat at the other side of the office, and one of them . . . was Black. I stuck my head over the Windows 1945 computer to inspect the intruder from afar. Their appearance seemed to be a cross between Kenan Thompson (from *Kenan and Kel*) and Whoopi Goldberg. I'll be honest: I didn't know if it was a guy or girl, but it didn't matter – I needed to take a closer look. I walked over to the new posse with an assured urban swagger and introduced myself. They were all friendly enough, but the mystery man (turns out he was more Kenan, less Whoopi) was in the middle of another conversation, so we exchanged nothing more than a brief flicker of eye contact. When I sat back down, I couldn't quite process my emotions. Was I jealous that another Black guy had entered my exclusive members' club? Was I threatened by the prospect that he would take the one spot reserved for a Black guy in the office and boot me back out into the bleak reality of beans and pasta? Or was I simply . . . excited?

I didn't have much time to work out my feelings towards my new nemesis because after a couple of weeks he had become my boss. I had managed to wriggle my way into becoming a writer on the daily live show. Technically we had a few bosses, but my Black boss was in charge of filling one and a half hours of TV with fresh and exciting content every day. Like any BAFTA-winning writer, I decided to fill my one and a half hours with memes from Twitter. However, unlike Twitter, to play memes on TV they needed to be approved – which meant showing my boss. I remember the day it happened: I had three memes opened on three tabs and the boss sat next to me, ready to approve or reject my hours of blood, sweat and scrolling. He snorted at the first one (probably something with a cat in it), didn't say anything at the second one, and then we came to the third meme. I can't remember exactly what it was, but I'm almost certain it would have been of a Black guy saying something hilarious before falling over and the cameraman bursting into that hysterical laughter only Black people do. As soon as I pressed play, we were both gone. We erupted into absolute fits of laughter. People were gathering round the computer to get a glimpse at whatever comedy masterpiece we'd just witnessed, but they'd leave shortly after because they didn't get it. I can't explain why only we found it funny, but in that moment it was like we were communicating through our laughter. I knew in that very second that my boss, Trent, would become my friend for life.

In the days that followed, Trent and I became inseparable.

We seemed to be constantly laughing at stupid videos on Twitter. We'd throw quick comical glances at each other whenever someone in the office made a comment with a racial twang, and very soon we were going round each other's houses to watch old clips of Dave Chappelle on YouTube or to listen to 2000s R&B. Through my friendship with Trent, I found a sense of belonging I'd never experienced before. All the typical eye-roll moments of a mostly white workplace didn't seem to matter any more because there was someone there to share them with. I liked work before, but I loved it now because I had a friend who I connected with on a deeper level. It was a unique connection forged by our unique experience in the workplace, and one that led to a very unique kind of joy (and probably a few complaints to HR because of the noise). Trent is no longer my boss – he's now one of the most incredible friends I could wish for and will soon be part of my own production company. And yes, I am very much looking forward to deciding how he gets paid.

I think I may have gone a tad overboard on the evidence bit of my point-evidence-explain, but, hey, you asked for it. Ultimately, Black joy for me is the connection we have to other Black people because of our joint experience on this planet. Black joy is laughing a little bit louder when we are together or even crying a little bit harder. It is the excited lurch you feel in your soul when you realize someone you barely know understands exactly what you have been through. Black joy is the flood of relief you get when you realize you were never really alone. Black joy is wonderful, it is special, it is magical. Some people find it at school, some people find it travelling, some people find it at home, but I found it in the workplace.

(With Trent, not the potato guy, by the way.)

FIND YOUR OWN JOY

Pick up the phone, call your work bestie and let them know you appreciate them.

66 Black joy for me is the connection we have to other Black people because of our **joint experience on this planet** **99**

Oxymorons and Other Lies
Literature as love

Faridah Àbíké-Íyímídé

WRITER

oxymoron | ˌɒksɪˈmɔːrɒn |

noun

A figure of speech whereby seemingly contradictory words make sense when placed together (e.g. deliberate mistake)

A Black child with a learning disability who loves to read, born into a world of words she cannot decipher, a language that bears no resemblance to the one she hears her family speak at home, and books whose characters look nothing like her

I used to hate reading. But I have always loved stories. These may not seem like statements that belong together, but to me oxymorons like this sum up my ongoing relationship with books and reading.

While a logophile or a linguist might take issue with referring to anything but words and phrases as oxymorons, I believe we often apply this sentiment to people. We make assumptions about who a person is and what they are capable of, and we suggest that their existence is contradictory to a hobby or even a career path. I was once told by a teacher that I shouldn't study English literature at university, that people like me don't do subjects like that. What he really meant was: working-class Black girls and 'good' degrees don't mix well. Faridah the English student, to him, was an oxymoron. This was apparent in his tone and the words that followed that statement. Of course, there is no such thing as a 'good' degree or a 'bad' one. What he was suggesting was wrong and influenced by his own prejudices. But this is a 'despite' essay. An essay about the way I found joy in reading *despite* my circumstances and *despite* the people who told me I couldn't – like that teacher. However, you should know this didn't just start with me wanting to prove people wrong. I should probably explain myself more, but in order to do that I need to go back to the beginning, to before I was born, to a different time and place where language and books carried an entirely different meaning to entirely different people.

My mum was born in 1968, eight years after Nigeria gained independence. She was raised by her aunt and grandmother, as her own mother – my grandma – was still a child herself. My mum grew up without siblings in a village in Nigeria, falling in love with books as a way to escape and cope with how lonely her childhood was. But her extended family looked down on her, seeing her as the child of an 'olodo'.

olodo | o-lo-do |

adjective

An insult to describe someone of low intelligence

A word used to mock and hurt people whose brains perceive the world differently. Being different isn't a bad thing, but using slurs to insult those you do not care to understand is.

My mum could not read Yoruba, the language that was primarily spoken in her tribe before colonization, but she could read English and devoured everything from classics to romance novels. She'd dream of other worlds and go on adventures with characters she considered to be her fictional siblings. These fictional worlds were real to her (another oxymoron) and brought her so much joy.

Whenever my mum tells me stories of her childhood, she'll mention how her aunt and her grandmother always encouraged her reading and education, ignoring the naysayers who tried to convince them that she was a lost cause and would amount to nothing, like my grandma. Despite being surrounded by those who spat spiteful words of discouragement at her when she'd struggle in school, my mum, with the help of the few who did believe in her, held on to her love of books and did the things her own mother was never allowed to do.

I fell in love with stories because of my mum and her love of reading and storytelling. She'd sing nursery rhymes, recite the folklore her grandmother passed down to her – such as 'Orí ati Olájùmoké', a story about a spoiled princess and a cunning spirit – and read books to me when I couldn't read them myself.

I used to feel as though reading was like going on a difficult voyage through a strange, dark forest. I was convinced that everyone else had secretly been given a map of how to navigate their way through, and whoever was in charge of distributing the maps had forgotten to give me mine. I was left to wander, lost and weaving through unfamiliar words and shapeshifting letters.

Unlike my mum, I struggled with English. I struggled to understand what words meant on my own. I hated quiet reading time at school, and I hated being told off by teachers for the way I read words aloud, stumbling over sentences, mixing up Ds with Bs, and how slow I was in comparison to other kids my age. Because I generally did well in school, they didn't understand why I had such awful spelling and grammar. They'd call me lazy or say I wasn't trying hard enough. In another context, they might've called me an olodo, like so many people called my grandma.

My mum would argue back and tell them how bright I was, how much I loved stories, how I just needed time to find my way through the weeds of vowels and consonants that tripped me up and the tangled thorny branches that moved the lines about the page and made it difficult to focus.

And indeed, eventually I'd pick up a story and the words would still take some time to digest, but they'd begin to make sense and pull me in. Suddenly, I found myself being able to escape too.

My mum once told me how teachers would ask if English was actually my first language, or whether I was really born in Africa. My mum assured them that I'd only ever lived in England, but they weren't so convinced. It was as if they had seen me struggling and assumed I lacked intelligence and therefore could not be English. It's interesting because when a white child struggles in school, they are often tested for learning disabilities. But me? When I struggled, I must've been from somewhere else.

To them, a smart African girl was an oxymoron.

To them, 'Nigerian' and 'slow' were synonyms.

synonym | ˈsɪnənɪm |

noun

A word that has the same meaning as another word, for example, *shut* is a synonym of *close*

Occasionally used when ignorant people stereotype and demean a minority group by acting as though the stereotype is literal, for example, using *African* to mean *unintelligent*

I think anyone can be a reader, but there are so many external factors that stop it from happening.

We are often taught in school which books are good and which books are bad. We are taught that books by old dead white people are the pinnacle of literary brilliance, and the modern books with slang or pictures or characters with Black and brown skin aren't good enough.

But that isn't true – not in the slightest. Good books are whichever ones that pull you in. They are books that make you smile or build on things you're already interested in learning. A good book is whatever you decide it is.

People are also deterred from reading because of what others tell them they are capable of. My mum and I both had people in our lives who told us we could do it, but not everyone is so lucky. Unlike my mum and me, no one fought like that for my grandma.

Many years ago, I came across the word 'dyslexia' when talking to one of my friends who had recently been diagnosed with it. She told me that it meant she struggled with reading and writing – and just school in general.

Despite relating to that in some way, I never even thought that that could be me.

You see, just like in books, people like me are under-represented in studies on learning disabilities. A lot of science has focused on how dyslexia presents itself in white children, so many Black people can go their entire lives not knowing that the reason they struggled in school or always hated reading is because of this thing no one thought to mention – because they didn't fit the already biased research or the pre-established ideas of what a dyslexic individual looks like.

It took me years of teachers ignoring my difficulties to finally search for the answers myself. I went to get a preliminary test, which would show whether I had any possible traits associated with dyslexia.

I passed with flying colours.

I then took a test with an educational psychologist who, after a series of exams, finally told me what I'd started to strongly suspect: that I was dyslexic and that the signs had probably always been there, but that teachers had never thought to look for them. Instead, they chose to believe I was lazy.

I think, truthfully, many teachers have grown used to seeing dyslexia represented in only one type of person, when really anyone can be dyslexic.

I am Black and dyslexic – something that is treated like an oxymoron but isn't.

So many dyslexic young adults, many of whom have not yet been given a diagnosis, are taught to see books as the enemy – as something that they'll never be able to enjoy.

All of this got me thinking about my grandma and her struggles with school and the things I'd heard about her. I asked my mum one day, 'Do you think anyone in our family is also dyslexic?' What I really wanted to ask was, 'Do you think Grandma is?' My mum said she wasn't sure; it wasn't something that people really discussed in Nigeria. If you're bad at school, you're seen as unintelligent and that's that. People rarely think that there might be something else going on.

I don't think this is unique to Nigeria – I think this is a problem all around the world. People assume there is one way to learn and those who can't learn in that one way are somehow failures.

There is more than one way to learn and there is also more than one way to read a book. As I said earlier, I used to hate reading. But I have always loved stories. I loved hearing my mum tell me Nigerian folktales, or even just her making up stories on the spot. I loved sitting in class and hearing other students read aloud. I loved when my teachers would read to us. I've always enjoyed telling stories myself. And now, as an adult, things haven't changed so much. I love audiobooks, I love graphic novels, I love poetry.

There are people out there who will claim that the only true way to be a reader is to:

1. Read books that are in paperback or hardback form.
2. Read books by certain kinds of authors.

And I'd say to them: did you know that physical books are a modern form of storytelling? Before, the oldest form of storytelling is oral storytelling that got passed down from generation to generation.

story | ˈstɔːri |

noun

An account of imaginary or real people and events told for entertainment

Something that is valid in all formats whether that be book form, audio, with pictures, in verse – whatever you wish it to be

Something that can be enjoyed by *everyone* regardless of their background

It can be hard to know where to start when it comes to reading. There are hundreds of millions of books out there – not to count the stories that haven't been written down. I'm a firm believer that everyone has a book out there for them. It might take a while to locate that book, but I believe it exists.

There are stories that make us readers, and I have a few that really changed the way I saw books. I'm someone who went from hating books and hardly reading them to reading so many in a year.

Dyslexic bookworm – another apparent oxymoron.

People will always try to tell you who they think you are. They'll tell you what you are and aren't capable of before you've even had the chance to dream it. They'll put your name next to something and claim it is an oxymoron – something that should not make sense together. However, the thing about oxymorons is that two seemingly opposing words or sentiments that aren't meant to work in conjunction magically do: *awfully good, bittersweet, barely dressed.*

According to many people, those who are neurodivergent or have learning disabilities, like me, aren't meant to find joy in reading. We aren't meant to become authors. We aren't meant to graduate or get a degree. But here we are doing it anyway. Like oxymoronic words, we exist in conjunction with our many hobbies and talents.

We are capable of everything and anything.

We can all be awfully good at what we're passionate about – it isn't magic or luck.

We can also be pretty bad at things that still make us happy.

At the end of the day, that's what matters the most – what we find joy in, especially in times of adversity.

Writing and reading bring me joy. In a book there is no limit to who or what you can be. In a world where people try to tell you what you are capable of, stories do the opposite. Fiction gives me the freedom to live an infinite number of lives and travel to an infinite number of places. Stories entertain, they inspire, they are sources of joy. Most importantly, they show us that we are capable of anything.

joy | dʒɔɪ |

noun

A feeling of great pleasure and happiness
Being able to escape into a book
Writing a story for yourself and others to escape into
Whatever you define it as

FIND YOUR OWN JOY

Look up the poem 'Still I Rise' by Maya Angelou. The best thing about poetry, especially Maya Angelou's poems, is that they are short and powerful. You can feel both accomplished and empowered in finishing the poem, especially if you struggle with words. Internalize her message: when the world tries to bring you down, still you rise.

" Stories entertain, they inspire, they are sources of joy. Most importantly, they show us that **we are capable of anything** "

I Don't Need No Man

Black Pride and me

Lauryn Green

STUDENT

At the impressionable age of nine, I sang along to 'Independent Women' by Destiny's Child like I was a grown woman with three kids and bills to pay. My *I don't need no man* mindset materialized early – thirty per cent because I was a little girl who wanted to be grown and seventy per cent because I am a raging homosexual. In my formative years, I wanted to replicate the amazing women in my life and become wholly self-sufficient.

As I emerged into early adolescence, this guise of 'self-sufficiency' began to morph into a deeply suppressive state of mind. I was navigating secondary school, insecure and frightened, like we all are at that age, but so, *so* determined not to show it. I pushed away every atom of my identity solely because I wanted to appear resilient and strong. *I don't need no man* turned into *I don't need nobody*. To me, being strong meant showing no weakness.

Black people are often depicted as 'strong'. For our ancestors, this strength was a question of survival, utilized to mitigate their suffering and fight for the right to exist. In a more contemporary sense, the term 'strong Black woman' has become a source of liberation for some, who find strength in spite of oppression and the many hurdles encountered through Black women's act of everyday existence. Many still wear the label like a badge, an affirmation reminding us to stay grounded and dedicated to our goals. However, over time, adjectives like 'strong' and 'resilient' have taken on a hue that is not inherently positive. Black women in particular must be strong, but not *too* strong, confident but not *too* confident, lest we get labelled as aggressive or other less favourable terms. There is a certain filter through which this strength must be presented, a lens that has not been constructed by ourselves but by others to mould us into something palatable.

During my formative years, the more I started to feel low, the more I hid it. Words like 'strong' and 'resilient' felt bound to me, like thorns in my skin, and we were inseparable, regardless of how much it hurt.

As a teenager, the essence of me felt like an extremely fragile equilibrium. Less like balance and more like chaos. When I started to realize that I was queer, I was presented with another identity conundrum and another facet of myself I felt I had to suppress. I felt like I was constantly oscillating between the constituent parts of my identity, as if they were entirely mutually exclusive and I had to pick one to adopt as my own. I couldn't be of Jamaican heritage *and* queer (I'd heard Buju Banton's homophobic anthem 'Boom Bye Bye' one too many times in this lifetime, boy). I couldn't be Black *and* mentally ill. In my mind, the 'ands' had to become 'ors', and I was a frantic youth, desperately trying to grasp some sense of stability. The lack of a Black queer presence in my immediate surroundings made me retreat deeper into my mind. I became withdrawn and insecure, adamant that I did not need to ask for help. Social media became a way to express my attractions in an immaterial world without judgement. Before that point, it was *inconceivable* that there could be people who looked like me basking in their queerness and being unabashedly committed to both their inner essence and outer presentation. It helped me recognize that self-acceptance was a lifelong pursuit and one that I just needed a push to commence myself.

This push came from an event that I will remember fondly for the rest of my life. In June of 2018, a tweet showed up on my timeline. 'History take the stage,' it read, and I realized that it was a promotional video for Black Pride, an event I had not heard of prior to that day. I clicked on it, curious and admittedly quite excited. A hand placed a mug on a desk, and as the camera panned up I was blessed with the sight of Lady Phyll in her ethereal beauty, staring dead into the camera. Her voice was both gentle and assertive, and I remember feeling as if I was in the room with her as she spoke. I knew that she meant every single word. As the video proceeded, I saw an array of queer people of colour speaking fearlessly to the camera, to me. I was in awe. None of these beautiful individuals appeared to be afraid or ashamed. And there was a revolutionary power in that, in their act of being themselves. I googled Lady Phyll, desperate to know more about this person. I read about how much she cares about Black queer collectivism, how she felt inspired to help Black queer youth for the better. I read about the conception of Black Pride, how it had rapidly become Europe's largest celebration for LGBTQIA+ people of colour. I realized that my Black queer predecessors had paved the way for me to exist in today's epoch. It was incredibly grounding, and ironic that social media, which I had previously used as a means of escaping reality, had brought to my attention something that I needed. I knew once the video ended that I had to attend this event. Fear has a concrete ability to prevent us from delving into unknown territory and I didn't want to let it.

Unfortunately, I didn't know any other queer people of colour at that point. However, I *did* know a couple of open-minded people who I felt would be comfortable accompanying me. I sent my friend Eden a minute-long voice note tentatively asking her to come with me, assuring her that you didn't have to be queer to attend, that it would be like a festival. Listening back to that voice note now makes me laugh because I sound like I'm nervously trying to persuade my mum to let me stay over at my friend's house: 'We can get there for one and be back by six. You don't have to be gay to go, I don't think – bare people go just to support and that, you get me?' Eden, because she is an absolute elite babe, was completely down to come with me and to this day

I am grateful for her willingness and support.

The night before 8 July 2018, I set an alarm for 6 a.m. even though I was leaving at noon. Embarrassingly, I had prepared for the day like it was a job interview: background research on the event (i.e. YouTube vlogs from previous years), a mental script to recall if my parents asked me about it, and, lastly, an outfit. I was frenetically worried about how I was going to present myself. Should I wear a shirt or is that too obvious? Will people on the street look at me and know where I'm going if I wear these trousers? All trivial concerns, but it goes to show just how uncomfortable I felt about my sexuality and gender expression. I settled on something summery, neutral and . . . horrifically ugly. I looked like I'd googled 'festival outfit for men' and just run with the first result I saw.

Since Eden and I lived in the same borough, we decided to travel to Vauxhall together. There we were: two Black girls off to their first Pride, Eden looking as stylish as ever and me looking like I was on my way to Coachella. We sat on the top deck, and every time someone new came upstairs we would make bets on whether or not they were attending Black Pride. Our criteria looked something like this:

1. Black or a person of colour

2. Some form of colourful attire (bonus if it was rainbow-themed)

3. Glitter, even if just a sprinkle

4. A certain energy (what this energy was I still don't know)

Retrospectively, I think this was all a product of my nerves. There was a tense jitteriness that shrouded the entire journey there, and this extended into full-blown anxiety when we reached our destination. I wore sunglasses throughout the entire event, afraid people would be able to look into my darting eyes and know I was the babiest of baby gays – not even fresh out the womb. I still very much consider myself a baby gay now, so you can imagine how novel it was to me at the age of seventeen. I was trying (and probably failing) to act cool, as if Black Pride was just something that I attended every year, that I was used to seeing such a magnitude of queer people in one space.

Suffice to say, my trepidation was unnecessary, because the second we entered the park I felt an immense sense of comfort. There were *so* many people that I was well and truly speechless. My mind had trouble registering the fact that the vast majority of them were queer, like me, that they had a similar heritage, that they were here in this space with an unbridled exuberance, laughing and dancing. Nothing was more emancipating than this moment, when for the first time I felt I had found my community.

I was immediately struck by the diversity of Black Pride. I

saw people who were young, old, a Black lesbian couple with a child. In a way, I felt that I was viewing the past, present and future all at once. For the first time in my life, I saw a version of a world that I felt I could be myself in, one I wanted to exist in. On the bus there, Eden and I had met two people of similar age who were both also visiting Black Pride for the first time and we were all navigating this new experience together. We all walked around aimlessly for a while, talking and drinking in the beauty of the day.

There is *always* something to do at Black Pride. Eden and I observed the various booths around the park and made it our mission to go to as many of them as possible. Each one was centred around a different topical issue or organization supporting LGBTQIA+ people of colour. We sat and listened to older individuals speak about their lives and experiences, and I was both inspired and deeply moved. I took as many of the free handouts as I could, and by the end of the event I was brandishing enough leaflets, lanyards and rainbow fans to set up my own stall. I was really moving like a tourist that day. There was also a stage with live performances and my biggest regret is not staying there longer. (Granted, I made up for it the following year!)

Around an hour after we had arrived, a reporter stopped us to ask us some questions. We were all surprised that we were approached, but we went along with it because he seemed important and it was exciting. The reporter asked why we thought Black Pride was such an important event and why it should co-exist with London Pride, as well as how we were finding the day so far. I am sure that I stumbled my way through some semi-coherent response about feeling comfortable in the space and how it was my first time at any Pride. It felt foreign and even slightly disconcerting to be asked about my identity and I remember hoping that our answers wouldn't get published in case people in my immediate circle saw the piece and recognized me. I still have no clue where our interview ended up!

I think about these same questions now. Why *is* Black Pride needed? To answer, I need only to think about how exhilarating it was to be at Black Pride at that age, to feel validated by the community. Black Pride gives queer people of colour the ability to *be* without fear of judgement or ridicule, and there's something liberating about the mutual enjoyment of its attendees, knowing that the infectious high energy is genuine. At Black Pride, you are never alone. You feel embraced by the arms of thousands solely by being in that space. You feed off the joy of others, and I can't stress how vital this is for people who are just finding their way in the world.

I *really* didn't want to leave, but we had to go (people with curfews get it). I sat on the bus experiencing a sense of camaraderie. I was inspired by the people I had met and all the booths I had visited. Eden and I had made friends, too, and to this day I am still close with one of them as we ended up attending the same university. I wore the rainbow lanyards that I had collected with pride the entire journey home, no longer caring if people saw. Nothing external mattered at this moment, because I was at ease with myself and I didn't want anything to rupture that. When I got home, I rushed to my bedroom and immediately hung the lanyards on my closet door (this is not a metaphor). They're still there today, acting as a sentimental reminder of one of the most fulfilling days of my teenage life.

Something shifted from that day onwards. I began to re-evaluate the patterns I had grown used to – particularly those relating to my perception of 'strength'. I was reminded of the people of Black Pride. I realized that strength had less to do with 'faking it till you make it' and suppressing everything that felt uncomfortable, and more to do with acceptance. Acceptance that I could exist as me without having to categorize myself, that to feel wasn't 'weak', that I didn't have to prove myself to anyone. Acceptance that there was nothing shameful in asking for help. I began to treat myself with more compassion.

Three years later and I'm still alive. As I leave my teenage years behind, I ponder over whether or not I wish things had been different. What would I say to nine-year-old me? To thirteen-year-old me? To seventeen-year-old me? I'd say that it is OK if you don't think you have figured everything out. That most people never do. That your identity is beautiful, and one day you will find strength in every element of it. That there is no shame in being who you are. And above all else, I'd say to be bold.

FIND YOUR OWN JOY

Put on your favourite outfit – the outfit that makes you feel free and beautiful – and DANCE!

" Your identity is beautiful, and one day you will find strength in every element of it **"**

My Ancestors Whisper in the Trees
Finding solace in nature

Melz Owusu

ACADEMIC & FOUNDER OF THE
FREE BLACK UNIVERSITY

Illustration by Chioma Ince

I am south-east London born and raised. I am used to big buildings, grey concrete, and the hustle and bustle this city thrives on. But, since I was very young, I have always had a whispering fascination with nature. I was struck by its beauty, its power to transform seedlings into rooted and strong trees that bear such vibrant fruits that nourish our souls. It amazed me how the trees were always so brave, that they let their leaves fall and stand naked in the autumn and winter, trusting in Mother Earth, in self, that those leaves would be replenished and even more beautiful in the spring. Nature is divine. I would stand in astonishment at the daily miracle of how the beautiful and mighty sun set over London every single day. I often found myself perplexed as to why the whole city didn't just stop to look up at its magnificence and instead continued to focus on the dreariness of the pavement.

For many of us Black Brits, the countryside can feel like a foreign world. As we grow older, it is not uncommon to become accustomed to other cities across Europe and the rest of the world before we explore the natural beauty around us. I got to know cities such as Berlin, Lisbon and New York like the back of my hand before I started to explore how I could connect with nature closer to 'home'. This is not said to place any value judgement on how we spend our time – listen, enjoyment is a must. However, the limits that the pandemic forced upon us made me look back into my inner self, my inner child, and ask where my fascination began. So I embraced the outdoors.

I am not here to kid myself or anyone else: I would have much preferred to be out on a beach in Salvador sipping on a sweet caipirinha or watching the sunset from a beautiful white villa at the highest point of Santorini. But it was lockdown in Babylon, and I had to find joy in what I could. The British countryside and the nature reserves near my home became a real solace for me on both a physical and spiritual level. Now, now, I know this may sound dead. Like, *Melz, allow it.* But, honestly, the peace, tranquillity, quality of air and produce that can be found around us is stunning. I find it a travesty that it took so long for me to engage with the outdoors in a meaningful way. The replenishing and healing power of nature on both the mind and the body is what I believe every single Black person confined to these borders deserves, and needs, to experience.

Racialized capitalism means that this is often an indulgence reserved for the white and wealthy, and now I understand why. It is a privilege that can do so much to support health that the limited access Black people have to such spaces, and the lack of belonging we may experience when occupying them, only serves to worsen the well-being of our community.

The irony is that we come from lineages of people that worshipped the land: our ancestors venerated deities of the

"The replenishing and healing power of nature on both the mind and the body that can be found in the nature around us is what **I believe every single Black person confined to these borders deserves, and needs, to experience**" waters and gods of the Earth. Nature was always seen as divine, sacred; we were all just an extension of this blessed nature. This idea of oneness, and a reverence for the power of nature, can be found in precolonial traditions right across Africa and the diaspora. In the Ifa tradition (which originated in Yorubaland, modern-day Nigeria), Oshun is the goddess of water, and she can be found at all the rivers and lakes where fresh water flows. She is also the goddess of beauty and all that is sweet in life. Across the world, people of African descent travel to places of natural beauty, and where the rivers flow they give up offerings and venerate Oshun. Oshun is honoured as a deity in traditions that travelled through the passage of the transatlantic slave trade from the African continent into the 'New World', where they are still being observed today – in practices such as Candomblé in Brazil, Vodou in Haiti and Santería in Cuba. To me, these traditions demonstrate a defiance of all sense of space and time. They display the undying power that is held in Blackness, and the ability for sacred knowledge to travel with us wherever we go.

When I moved to Cambridge in October 2020 to begin studying for my PhD, I found the natural beauty in and around the city to be breathtaking. I spent evenings stargazing for hours on end, free of London's intense light pollution. I went for walks that took me down winding country roads

Chioma Ince

"That is
what nature
offers me:
**total
embodiment**"

and to waters that looked clear enough to drink. Cows and sheep were roaming and grazing on open fields; it just felt like *life* was in every direction. I took a staycation to write in a cabin not too far from the city, and I was able to look out to unending fields and weaving waters. The joy I felt was palpable; I feel it rushing back as I write now.

What a blessing it was to be surrounded by the power and beauty of nature. The world was at a standstill, and so it almost felt like it was not my duty to note how much time had elapsed. I was able to be present in every hallowed moment. As I meditated by the softened waters, I felt called to be present with my body, to be present with every breath that passed my lips, with every blade of grass I sat upon, and with all that was around me. That is what nature offers me: total embodiment. To feel at one and at peace with myself and all that surrounds me, to recognize that nature is also a divine part of me.

As a queer, Black, working-class, trans person, the countryside may seem like the most contrasting canvas for an identity and body like my own. However, it has become one of the places I am able to feel most in my body and closest to my homeland and ancestors when on these shores. I envision a future in which all Black people from across the country can experience the benefits that the countryside can bring. It can honestly be a lifeline.

I come from a long lineage of farmers in Kumasi, Ghana. My ancestors worked the land to bring forth a bounty of fresh fruit and root vegetables to nourish themselves and the community. When I think about what it would have taken to tend to a farm like theirs back in the day, I find it remarkable that they were able to do what they did. A connection to the land was vital: there was no modern machinery or weather projections to rely on – only the knowledge that had been passed down and the connection they were able to make with the land. My great-grandfather was a very spiritual man and he would pour libation on to the clay and soil to respect his own ancestors each day. I am sure they supported him in cultivating the earth and making timely decisions to ensure that our family farm was as abundant as it could be. Season to season, we grew and harvested cocoa beans, plantain, cocoyam, cassava, mangos, pineapples, bananas and so much more. My mum has told me many stories of how she would sit at the farm on sweltering days as my great-grandmother cut up pineapple and papaya into delicate pieces for her and her siblings to eat, so the adults could get to work. It's no wonder that I find such a resonance with nature and the land. It is home. In most precolonial spiritual traditions, before we approach the orishas and deities, our ancestors are our first port of call. They are our guides into the spirit world, and our supporters through life.

In Cambridge, when I would gaze at the stars and walk for hours on end, I would always speak. Speak to the trees and the waters; speak even to the air that I breathed. I was asking if my ancestors were well. Asking for their guidance in all that I do in this lifetime. Taking them offerings of fresh fruit to lay by the trees and pouring libation on to the soil, so that they would know I wanted to give to them just as much as they continued to give to me. Nature is worthy for her beauty alone, but these spiritual and ancestral elements take us further into sacred power and joy beyond the limits of Western science. It's a joy that our ancestors observed; perhaps they would surely be glad to know that this is how we also choose to remember and connect with them. I believe that when we speak to nature, she speaks back. The voice of our ancestors, the energies of deities, the connection to the most divine parts of ourselves. A journey through nature is a journey back towards self, and I believe the truest essence of joy can only be found on that journey. Joy is within us, not outside of us. On the journey to self, I am so grateful to be able to learn more about those who came before me as I listen to the ways they communicate with me through their whispers in the trees.

In a world where Blackness and death continuously have too close a companionship, joy can often be difficult to find. And when we find it, it can feel too fleeting to hold on to. This asks us to call into question the belief that physical death is the end of all life. I vehemently do not believe this, and neither did our ancestors prior to colonization. Energy never dies. All the loved ones that we have lost can be found and connected with as we seek out the alternative truths of nature. Blackness lives on in many forms, embodied and unembodied. Presence with nature has taught me this.

I will leave you with a proverbial message from my ancestors, one that I heard whispering to me through the trees. They reminded me that fire is a cleansing force. Without the fire that beams down from the sky, we would be stricken with infertile land, as the sun is what causes the crops to grow. If the world is on fire, it is no different from the sun scorching the ground at the height of the harmattan. If the sun did not scorch, then the land would not be able to hold all the water needed for the crops to grow when the rainy season came. So, while in many ways our world is in flames, and despite how intensely the heat bears down on us, we must continue to do the work of finding joy, so that we may nourish ourselves to grow a bountiful future.

FIND YOUR OWN JOY

Find a piece of nature – anything from a plant in your room to somewhere deep in the woods – and try to be as present with it as you can. Empty your mind of all that the day holds, all worries, all fears, and practise presence. Listen closely to the messages held within the beauty and sacredness of nature. Now write down and reflect on what feelings arise.

Black FM
My connection to Black radio

Henrie Kwushue
PRESENTER & DJ

My journey into radio started with a paradox. I had always wanted to make people smile, but I was cripplingly shy. It was hard for me to make conversation with people in real life, so you can only imagine being on the radio – having to speak to hundreds, maybe thousands, of people. I used to feel like I had nothing to say, but eventually I found my voice. It was in finally overcoming my shyness and throwing myself into radio that I was able to feel Black joy.

My earliest memory of personally connecting with radio was when I was around ten years old, listening to a presenter duo on Choice FM. I remember loving their confidence and the fact that they were able to bounce off each other so well. My young brain was asking questions like: Do they have scripts? How do they think of what to say off the cuff? Do they come up with their jokes on the spot? In between their chat, they were playing all the music I knew and loved from TV, and I know it sounds silly but it blew my mind.

Funnily enough, we didn't have the radio on that much in my house. Instead, a lot of the music I consumed was from the TV. I was the kind of kid who used to cry when the new N-Dubz and Chip videos came on – my love for the UK scene is deep-rooted like that. I feel like a lot of us who were born in the 1990s who grew up in London have the same story of watching endless SBTV F64s on YouTube and switching back and forth between Channel U and MTV Base (if you had Sky).

As a younger, I thought I was a lyrical connoisseur. You know that feeling when you hear a bar that makes your head explode and you have to reload the whole song ten times and then replay that specific bar another five? That's how I fell in love with music. The done thing at the time was to get out your Nokia or Samsung phone and Bluetooth your favourite songs to your friends in the playground, knowing full well you weren't allowed phones in primary school. It's a part of me that lives on with my love for music nowadays.

It's the same type of feeling I regularly have when I listen to radio. Growing up, I quickly realized that songs broke on radio well before they made their way to TV, so I would sit around waiting for my favourite artists' songs to premiere. In between songs, I'd be hanging on to every joke the presenters made. Because of this, I fell in love with the idea of presenting. Presenters had to be natural talkers, making a listener feel like they were speaking only to them, while also showing a passion for music. It was a skill I thought you needed superpowers to master.

We often see someone doing something we think is amazing but never consider the option of putting ourselves in their shoes, doing the same thing. That was me for a very long time. It was important for me to make that leap, converging the dream of being the Black babe on radio to *actually* being the Black babe on radio. I grew up listening to some pioneering

Black radio personalities over the years, from Trevor Nelson to Clara Amfo to Sarah-Jane Crawford to Sian Anderson. Hearing Clara on the radio for the first time was an incredible moment; having a dark-skinned, Black, Ghanaian hun on a mainstream station was breathtaking.

As a teenager, as much as I loved listening to everyone on the air, I was always seeking out someone who looked or sounded more like me. This, of course, was an impossible task – but it eventually became a beautiful lesson: sometimes the representation you're trying to find is YOU. Over time, I realized that having people to look up to in the industry was great, but I'd only become the best presenter I could be by being authentically myself. That way, the little Black girl at home listening to the radio, waiting desperately for the next premiere or even dreaming of being a presenter, would see that she only has to be herself too.

My broadcasting career started at Reprezent Radio, a youth-led community station based in south London. I had done work experience with them once when I was fourteen, and from there I had seen them nurture new talent, including Jamz Supernova, Snoochie Shy and Reece Parkinson. I wanted that for myself. Reprezent was a great way to segue into mainstream, paid radio gigs because it gave leeway for mistakes while nurturing character and talent that already exist within.

"Sometimes the representation you're trying to find is YOU"

My first opportunity in Black radio was given to me by No Signal: made by Black people for the masses. Before it became the success it is today, No Signal was the sister radio station to a huge Black-centric party called Recess. No Signal didn't have many followers; it was mostly for fun. They'd sometimes stream sets from the Recess parties so people could listen at home if they couldn't attend the event, and they'd host intimate parties too. It felt niche, like you were part of a bubbling underground scene. But when lockdown came about, all of that changed drastically; suddenly there was nothing to do and no scene to be a part of. Then the CEO of Recess and No Signal, Jojo Sonubi, called me up and asked if I'd like to host a show called NS10v10, where artist would go against artist with ten songs picked by their fans.

By this time, everyone had already discovered Versus, created by producer Swizz Beatz, in which two artists showcased their music using Instagram Live. Jojo was adamant that he wanted an experience that was audibly immersive for the audience, and he came to the conclusion that radio was the best way to do this. Without even thinking twice, I said yes. We were eventually able to get some famous people to be contestants on the show, such as sports pundit and former footballer Ian Wright and DJ Julie Adenuga, alongside artists like Kranium, Konan and Ray BLK. Our biggest show, one that I had the pleasure of presenting, was Wizkid versus Vybz

Kartel; Burna Boy even streamed it live from Nigeria on his Instagram and it hit a million listeners worldwide.

As our radio show got bigger, we realized we wanted to run like a proper station with daily content of at least ten hours. We also wanted to stand for something. As a small creative team, we decided to go for it. We went with a 'for us by us' approach, seeing as everyone involved was Black. We created a Black space that played the best in Black music, had the best Black guests and spoke about what's important to Black people. Eventually, we developed shows that tackled the Black Lives Matter movement and issues in the diaspora; shows that flaunted the best in new music; specialist shows from famous people; and, of course, NS10v10.

The history of Black radio in the UK is really interesting to me. Black British voices on the radio date from as far back as the 1940s, with Una Marson being the first Black female presenter and programme-maker on the BBC for a show called *Calling the West Indies*. During the Second World War, amid air raids in London, Una would still broadcast live because she understood the importance of reaching out to the rest of the diaspora in the capital so that their voices and concerns could be heard.

As time went on, Black voices and music remained underground in the world of radio, and with that emerged pirate stations (which were on the airwaves without a licence).

If you look online, you'll find a photo of Kiss FM in the 1980s, then a pirate station with a mostly Black workforce. It's what Black Brits needed for our music to be heard by the masses. Even James Brown thanked Kiss FM for contributing to his success, according to radio presenter Lindsay Wesker. More broadly, it allowed for the rise of jungle music, ragga, grime and all other genres that would have been seen as intrinsically Black, and therefore underground. It paved the way for presenters and artists alike, and many big names in the industry today came up on underground stations.

With new technology, there's been a lot of discourse about the future of radio and other traditional forms of broadcasting, with many people saying they're on the decline. But this discourse happens every decade, and if radio is still going strong in the era of Instagram Live and podcasting, then it's not going anywhere. A whole new Black station was built from nothing and amassed a huge audience during a pandemic.

It's so integral for Black people to have our own sphere in the world of radio, and for us to have longevity and ownership of it. In 2013, Choice FM, one of the UK's only 'legal' radio stations that championed Black music (alongside Colourful Radio), was replaced by Capital Xtra. Boya Dee called it the 'end of an era'. However, it has been great to see that Capital Xtra has maintained Choice FM's ethos, with brilliant Black presenters such as Yinka Bokinni, Shayna Marie and Robert Bruce. Without it, Black music and Black voices might never have been as mainstream as they are today. Radio has been critical in platforming new music, artists, presenters and stories, and Black British radio has strengthened our identity. We deserve to have our own stake in these things. Pirate radio had us bubbling, but underground.

Since the inception of No Signal, I've felt like Black radio isn't going anywhere anytime soon. I love that we're at a place where Black creative content can be mainstream and get the shine it deserves. I'd love to see young Black people wake up one day and decide they also want to get into radio, even if it's something they'd never usually consider or, like me, were too shy to even think they'd make it in. I'm hoping for a future where Black radio is a normal part of society and can stand toe to toe with the conglomerates already in existence. My sincere wish is that Black radio continues to bring joy to everyone.

FIND YOUR OWN JOY

Tune into Black radio stations like No Signal and enjoy the music and banter they have to offer!

"It's so integral for Black people to have our own sphere in the world of radio, and for us to have **longevity and ownership of it**"

Chicken and Chips After School

How a girl gang allowed me to be my unfiltered self

Chanté Joseph

BROADCASTER

My best friend from secondary school, Charlotte, simply went by the nickname 'White Girl' when we were growing up. We laugh about it every time we catch up, but it was truly a testament to how diverse school was for us. At our girls' school in north-west London, most of the students were brown and Muslim. Cultures were respectfully shared and embraced, and we always had a deep appreciation for what each person's background allowed them to contribute. School was eerily quiet during Eid, and our class pictures were a sea of headscarves, a few coily afros and the odd white face. Black and Asian girls were not the minority in this space; we owned it. Unlike university, I didn't spend every day defending my very being or feeling inferior because of my Blackness. In my school, everyone had a story. There were no white protagonists – we were all the main characters.

Looking back through old Myspace accounts and photos from that time, I was reminded that at school my 'tag name' – as we called it back then – was 'Wifey SpongeBob'. I really enjoyed the cartoon and decided, briefly, to base my whole persona around it. On a non-uniform day, aged fourteen, I wore bright yellow jeans, a yellow SpongeBob T-shirt, yellow laces in my hair and a yellow SpongeBob scarf. I was a yellow vomit mess, but I loved every single moment. Crest Girls' – or John Kelly Technology College prior to academization – was the only place, for better or worse, where I could be my uninhibited self. The school has a powerful attachment to my family history: my mother, cousin and aunt all went to John Kelly and my late grandfather attended the boys' school. In a strange way, it felt like I was meant to go there and form the connections that I still reminisce about today. This dingy school-turned-academy provided me with a space to figure myself out and learn who I was outside of the white male gaze.

Turn back the clock. It's the start of Year 11 and we're in the newly refurbished toilets with unmarked red cubicle doors. 'Hello, I'm Chanté Joseph and this is *Interview Something Random*,' I say to the camera in my best BBC News voice, holding my water bottle like a microphone. 'On tonight's show, we have . . . Billy the spider!' Nyasha nervously pans to the sink where an enormous black spider rests. 'It's huge!' she squeals. 'So, um, what are you doing, Billy?' I say hastily, before Nyasha runs the tap and the spider scuffles out of the sink directly towards us, as if it's on the attack. We begin screaming, afraid to look at the beast, and run for dear life out of the toilets before descending into laughter. Watching videos from this era and hearing our clipping screams irritates my eardrums but also fills me with nostalgia. That was more or less what every schoolday was like: screaming, performing and, most importantly, genuine friendship.

Though we were a multicultural school, naturally we fell

into our groups. The Moroccans were a clique and so were the Somalis, the small group of Irish girls and so on – with some mixing in between. I was part of a small group of Black girls in my year: Jessica, Nyasha, Latoya and me. Though there would be arguments, we were more or less an inseparable bunch, and most of our schooldays were spent being loud and erratic together. In our small group, we learned and experienced a lot. It was our own small coming-of-age movie, our very own *Mean Girls* – but make it friendlier and more working class. Having a Black girl gang at school prepares you for the world in ways that textbooks can't.

In our small group, we dealt with body image, colourism, depression, self-harm and sexuality. We thought deeply about the politics of beauty and consoled each other through difficult family relationships and the daily traumas of growing up in broken homes. As eldest daughters, we all carried the weight of being forced to grow up quickly; we were second-in-command, raising and caring for our younger siblings without fathers who were living with us. We didn't bond over trauma, but it was something that allowed us to support each other. In some ways, we were robbed of being young and reckless, but when we were together we got to retreat into that state and just be teenagers. It was our freedom.

My memories from that time are bountiful. We'd all buy thick, black, figure-hugging trousers from the boutiques on Kilburn High Road and then pop a few shops down to Primark, where we'd pick up cheap pumps, adorning them with colourful laces that matched our hair bobbles. In the market across the road, we'd buy chunky fake diamanté earrings that would lose their shine as soon as we left the stall and metres of ribbon to tie in our hair. After a long day of trudging the high street, we'd dine at a chicken takeaway. Two greasy burgers and two bags of fries for £2 (before inflation ruined it for everyone) was an assured filling meal, albeit devoid of all nutrition.

Jessica, Nyasha, Latoya and I were thick as thieves in school and generally very troublesome. Nyasha was Zimbabwean and had been homeschooled prior to secondary, so naturally she was incredibly smart. She had endless energy and would always have the whole class and even teachers in fits of laughter with her unfunny jokes. She had the most emotional intelligence out of us all and, as the darkest in our group, inadvertently taught us about colourism and called us out on our problematic statements. She was also a self-confessed tomboy – I remember distinctly when she wore trainers with a dress to a fancy event we attended at the Brent Civic Centre, while the rest of us wore gowns and heels that were probably too high. Jessica, the diplomat of the group, was Angolan, spoke Portuguese and had a body to die for. She was reserved and easy-going – the person you could speak to when you needed to be perked up or wanted to laugh. And last but not least, Latoya, my fellow Caribbean, was the brains of the group – every English teacher's dream. She endlessly devoured novels, collecting new and intimidating words to add to her vocabulary like Sonic rings. We were the closest, spending so much time together that our parents couldn't tell our voices apart. I was always in admiration of Latoya; she didn't have to prove she was smart – she just was – and she probably understated a lot of her talents so as not to stand out too much.

Latoya recounts that our wits spared us the punishment we deserved for much of our heinous behaviour in school. One time in Year 11, our lofty PE teacher, Ms Ayles, was – as per usual – yelling at us. 'Girls, put on your PE kits!' she bellowed from afar. Naturally, we ignored her and continued nattering away about the food-tech coursework we were doing. Ms Ayles did not like being ignored, especially so blatantly. However, we were in our final year and felt like we ruled the school; we'd been there long enough to take risks and get away with it. She got closer, took a deep breath and roared: 'UHH, GIRLS, I SAID PUT ON YOUR PE KITS!' We collectively paused in disbelief and suddenly burst into uncontrollable laughter. How dare our PE teacher have the *audacity* to ask us to put on our PE kits during PE?

During lunchtime, if the hall was empty, we'd stage re-enactments of tabloid talk shows such as *Jerry Springer*.

Someone would volunteer a storyline and we'd have to act it out. Of course we'd always behave absolutely erratically, throwing chairs, howling and running around like headless chickens until we were told to shut up by tired teachers who could hear us screeching from their lounge. I had never felt freer than when I was pretending to be a woman whose husband (Latoya) was cheating on me with my eldest daughter (Nyasha). I'd collapse to the floor acting out my inconsolable grief suddenly – only snapping out of character when the bell rang to send us all to double science.

When we weren't acting, creating news reports or simply screaming for screaming's sake, we would sing constantly. Every day was an opportunity to create a new catchy song. When the teacher would implore us to stand behind our chairs before dismissing us in an orderly fashion, we'd belt 'CAN YOU STAND BEHIND YOUR CHAIR?!' to the tune of Whitney Houston's 'I Have Nothing'. We'd spend break times learning raps to battle each other at lunch, and I cannot help but think that had we been in the era of TikTok or even Vine, we'd have been stars. Most famous was a two-minute mash-up of songs we had produced over the years, which started as follows:

Oh my giddy giddy gosh, tell your mum to have a wash
Enter your phone number into my Nokia

Boom selecta you smell like shit
Ohh that's bad you smell like Grandad
Please, please you smell like rotten cheese
Cheese from your toes going up to my nose

It is easy building bonds with Black women – there is an unspoken understanding, an ancestral kinship that was formed long before we were thoughts in our parents' minds. Our group was far from perfect, but it taught me a lot about how the friendships you choose can bring so much unexpected happiness into your life when you most need it. Making friends as an adult is incredibly hard, and as someone with ADHD it is even harder. Rejection sensitive dysphoria, a condition that is common with ADHD, makes you fearful and averse to rejection – so much so that you limit the opportunities to experience rejection by never putting yourself out there. Inattentiveness and constant thrill-seeking also mean it can be hard to be present and active in relationships. In a school setting, where you are forced to make and build consistent connections, I found I was able to bond in ways that adulthood doesn't allow for. I have spent a lot of my short adult life chasing that same dynamic again. It was a privilege to have a singular group of people who had almost identical experiences to me and who were my biggest source of support.

"It is easy building bonds with Black women – there is an unspoken understanding, an ancestral kinship that was formed long before we were thoughts in our parents' minds**"**

The pandemic forced me back home to north-west London, and though I am once again living a stone's throw from the school, it now looks unrecognizable. Students in faded blue JKGTC jumpers aren't clamouring into frail huts that could just about weather the elements, like back when I was at school. The academization process means the school is now mixed and in a shiny new building devoid of personality (read: graffiti and crumbling exteriors). I pass it while running and miss the old days. I miss my friends, who have built new lives for themselves on the roads that time paved between us. However, I know that some friendships are not meant to last forever and that's OK. I cherish the memories and community we once had: the laughs, the back-of-the-bus banter, the partying, the songs, the screaming and, most importantly, the Black sisterhood they provided me with.

It is strange to think that one day we all logged out of Myspace and never logged back in again. We sent a final message on MSN Messenger, closed the box where the small green emoticons lived and heard that da-da-dum notification for the last time. It is also strange that, without knowing it, one day the gang – Jessica, Nyasha and Latoya and I – all went out for the last time and that was the end of our story. Looking back at my schooldays helps me to reconnect with a version of myself I sometimes forget: who I was before I first truly felt racialized in a negative way. I did not grow up with expectations of what it meant to be a Black woman; and from SpongeBob T-shirts, bad relaxer and even a strange stint in Year 9 of wearing contacts and claiming it as my true eye colour, to endless days spent laughing at bad jokes and singing songs, the sisterhood we had at school meant that we were all growing and accepting of each other. I was never an outcast.

FIND YOUR OWN JOY

Sometimes we don't realize the impact we've had on someone's life until they tell us about it. Why not reach out to an old friend and let them know you're thinking of them or remind the friends you do have that you love them dearly!

"The sisterhood we had at school meant that we were all growing and accepting of each other. **I was never an outcast**"

Intentionality as Praxis

How I create my own joy

Lavinya Stennett

CREATOR OF THE BLACK CURRICULUM

Growing up in the church, I heard joy spoken about as if it were a tangible gift, something you could receive. It sounded as easy as swiping right to approve and the feeling would be yours, forever. To me, this was a revelation. I knew joy was possible, but I didn't think that it was something that was sustainable or that you could own. For me at that time, joy was always something done to you in some incidental way – you sort of fell luxuriously into it.

As a child I was very aware of the things that brought me joy: playing outside with friends until late, going to family barbecues, getting my hair cornrowed in wavy patterns. I could easily count on the things that made me happy and indulge in them when I had the chance. But I also became accustomed to those things swiftly being taken away, especially when I came home with a head full of fresh braids without my parents' permission; I was made to sit down and take them out one by one. This led me to believe that my inner state was strictly guided by external events. I believed that my joy was determined by others, especially those in authority. My parents set a lot of rules, and as long as I followed those rules I could be happy.

As I got older, I started asking more questions. What even was joy? Was it the permanent grinning face of a Cheshire cat? The feeling of doing cartwheels after receiving great news? I was afraid that my perception of joy could change all of a sudden and that the experiences I'd once believed were 'joyful' were actually not. The more questions I had, the more unsure I felt, but I was soon to arrive at my answer.

Fast forward. I am in my second year at the School of Oriental and African Studies (SOAS) in London, aged twenty-one, and I am outraged. For the past three months, I have been working on a campaign called #ThatWay, which seeks to give students from low-income backgrounds backdated compensation for bursary funds after the university hadn't made them aware they were entitled to them. When I and another student officer realized that hundreds of students from low-income households were not receiving the funds, we were upset and disappointed, but not entirely surprised. I was so upset, however, that I spent my Christmas break planning how we could take over the management's office and demand change.

And so in March 2020 it begins. After many voice-note exchanges and secret meetings, around ten of us are persuaded that if any change is going to take place, we will have to work collectively and it will need to happen by force. With the backing of the student union, we start to prepare. Countless emails are sent, banners are painted and forums are held as we inform angered students about the issue. With growing awareness across the university, it is only right that we make the campaign official and get ourselves some

T-shirts that exclaim our disapproval of the issue.

In the days leading up to the occupation, our strategy is set, with the points where we will begin and end the protest coordinated. However, nothing can prepare us for the day it arrives. There is a nervous excitement in the air. We finish the first round of chants and begin to walk outside with our speakerphones to grace the SOAS steps. Remarkably, before we can even blink, management struts through the main doors, giving us the perfect opportunity to make our demands directly.

It's myself and two colleagues integral to the campaign – Chris and Comfort – who realize its success rests on this moment. We gear up on the spot and use our voices to articulate the issue of misallocated funds. The protest is joined and supported by international students, students who hear us all the way from the library, and even lecturers; we are there on the main staircase for hours. And it is joyful. Chris, Comfort and I are leant against the railings, bellowing through speakerphones in front of management, while being surrounded by other students, who are chanting and flashing the lights on their phones. The moment is a beautiful escapade of radical hope and unity between low-income, mostly Black students and allies for an outcome that will directly and tangibly impact many.

It feels very surreal, as if time is standing still. We are

in the moment and that in itself is liberating. Standing in the exact corridors where decisions are made on behalf of students, we feel triumphant as we reclaim the space and challenge the process of decision-making. When we wrap up, we can't stop talking about it. There is a palpable excitement in the air and that afternoon lecturers greet us with subtle nods of acknowledgement. By the evening, videos of the event are circulating. We know that the protest will go down in SOAS history. Two weeks later, after a few meetings as a result of the campaign, all of the students who are eligible for the bursary receive the funds they are owed.

Without a doubt, the experience was underlined by optimism as we were intentional about the outcome. It was exhilarating and completely necessary. Despite the risk of exclusion and our entire campaign being discredited by university management, we felt unified in a movement that gave us hope for social change. This hope was captured all across the university.

After that moment, and the more I experienced that feeling of giddiness and pride in seeing change, the less I believed that joy was external to reality. It wasn't something that was given and taken away. I came to accept joy as something that exists already – that is within our power to cultivate, shape and share. As with the #ThatWay campaign in university, my joy is something I can create intentionally.

"I came to accept joy as something that exists already – **that is within our power to cultivate, shape and share**"

Learning to see joy as something that was in my power to manifest – through my activism during my time at university – was followed by my journey into creating the Black Curriculum, a social enterprise aiming to embed the teaching of Black histories in schools and other arenas for education all year round. Founded in 2019, just before I graduated from university, it has become my world. In the early stages of setting up the Black Curriculum, I spent a lot of time searching for and defining the 'why': the purpose, the ultimate vision – which is to see every young person develop a sense of identity through Black history. I could see that our education system was rotating old ways of teaching, rather than investing in young people's learning. In discussions with Black friends, colleagues and other people, there was a shared experience of spending time in institutions that lacked interest in us, and of learning material that offered little hope. Finding and clinging on to the prospect of an uplifting experience in the midst of those places was futile because the wider mechanism was devoid of true understanding. The statistics on educational outcomes for Black students in secondary and higher education were bleak. The Black Curriculum therefore had to offer an alternative – or what I would describe as an antithesis – to social oppression. For us to counter the lack of hope, our vision, material and approach as a team had to be rooted consistently in reality and be uplifting, which is why I consider joy even more powerful as a shared experience.

The truth is that British society has not designed the space for unfiltered Black joy to exist. Racism by its nature makes joy a challenge, especially in education. Expressions of Black joy are often confined and policed. To exist loudly in joy as a Black person is a tricky business. It's almost as if you have to weigh up your options: express your joy or escape being mislabelled, abused or even killed. There is little safety in looking for joy externally. For our joy to be valid, it has to be unconditional and outlive our material conditions.

For us as activists, alternative ways of viewing the world when the present reality gives us little to be hopeful about can be made into a pleasant experience, especially when we set out with the intention to create a new reality. The people who share our ideas and drive forward our visions are part of the process of creating history too, which is why it is important to select your community with intention. The key is to mobilize and work with those you can share hope with – as there will be days when loneliness and pessimism set in.

So long as we have the internal tools to define what we'd like to see and set out to create that with purpose, we can make Black joy not just a possibility but a lasting experience that gives hope to the next generation.

FIND YOUR OWN JOY

On Sunday, sit down to plan out three hours of joy in the week ahead.

"We can make Black joy not just a possibility but a lasting experience **that gives hope to the next generation**"

In Harmony
An ode to stranger communities

Timi Sotire
JOURNALIST & EDITOR

Illustration by Jovilee Burton

Don't you just love concerts? Are there any words that perfectly capture the joy of seeing your favourite musical act in the flesh? Even though you've watched every single one of their music videos and live performances and never missed a social media post, their real-life presence hits you differently. You feel honoured to be sharing a concert hall with a talented artist you love and admire, surrounded by people who feel just as unworthy as you. You and your fellow concertgoers are filled with gratitude; there's a sense of humility that seeps into the atmosphere, bonding you all together as one.

Since my teen years, I've had a deep fascination with simply existing alongside strangers in these moments. As a young Black girl raised in Essex, being in groups that shared a common interest was one of the rare opportunities I had to be myself.

In secondary school, I was spotty and awkward, with a body that was changing faster than my mind could keep up with. Where most of my friends were talking about boys they dated or parties they attended, I was that one in the group who obsessed over books, who experienced the same elated sensation from achieving eighty per cent on a test as my friends did when they kissed their scrawny crushes. I thought my brain was wired incorrectly and I was never going to be like my peers. When you're a teenager, you forget there's a whole life outside of the brutalist-inspired tower blocks you're forced to attend five days a week, and it's easy to assume that school will set a precedent for the rest of your life. Among a sea of white faces, I was haunted by the possibility of always feeling like I didn't belong.

One day in 2010, everything changed. I was sitting with my family watching *The X Factor* at the boot-camp stage, and towards the end of the episode Simon Cowell put five random floppy-haired boys into a band, even though they had varying degrees of singing ability (I'm talking about you, Louis Tomlinson). Instantly, a fire ignited inside my prepubescent chest. 'I like where this is going,' I thought to myself, smirking as I watched the boys jump at Simon's good news. They called themselves One Direction. Every Saturday evening for the rest of the year, I was glued to the screen, watching the boys progress in the competition. I'd binge their weekly video diaries on YouTube, swooning as Zayn screamed 'Vas happenin'?', and start each morning googling their names on my BlackBerry Curve.

Eventually, they came in third place. I was heartbroken they didn't win, mainly because I'd used all my phone credit calling to vote for them. But, deep down, I knew they were destined for greatness. I wasn't aware of how much these five boys would define my life. They weren't just an *X Factor* act – they consumed my entire existence. They were the first thing I thought of when I woke up and the last thing

I thought of when I went to sleep.

I may sound like a teen-girl stereotype, but these boys genuinely ended up being my saving grace at twelve years old. Like most of us in school, I was constantly looking for ways to assimilate. Then One Direction came along, creating a real point of convergence with my classmates. Although I recognized that being the only Black girl in my friendship group meant that I would always be exposed to experiences they couldn't fathom, thinking about how we all loved One Direction made me feel like I could fit in. The joy this brought was unparalleled to me as a Black tween, and with time my obsession with these five boys showed me how much sharing fleeting moments with strangers would form a key part of my self-love journey.

My friends and I – Timi, Emily, Amy and Millie – called ourselves the 1D T.E.A.M. For months, we tried to see One Direction at meet-and-greets, to no avail. So, when their first UK tour was announced, we *had* to go. I thought I was dreaming when I saw the BBM from Amy telling us that she'd managed to get four tickets to see them at the Hammersmith Apollo.

One evening in early January, days before the concert, the 1D T.E.A.M. assembled in Millie's room to prepare. As 'What Makes You Beautiful' blared through Millie's speakers, the four of us stared blankly at the long piece of fabric we planned to use as a banner. We had tasked ourselves a week before to think of the wittiest phrase that we could paint on it. This, of course, ended up being '1D get in my pants'. We were twelve! Lusting over One Direction fuelled a nascent sexual desire ramped up by teenage hormones. Although juvenile and slightly objectifying, moments like these shaped the forms of sexual expression I appreciate today. As One Direction's tracklist boomed around us, the banner began to take shape. We used a lot of paint and way too much glitter and cut out photos of each band member to stick on it.

While Millie stapled her knickers on to the corner, thinking that it would bring '1D get in my pants' to life, I looked at my three friends and suddenly realized this was one of the few times I'd been at a friend's house after school, because my strict Nigerian parents didn't let me out much. I'd stopped asking them if I could hang out with my friends as I knew they'd say no, which in turn led to people no longer inviting me. This added to the isolation that I naturally experienced being the only Black girl in my friendship group. Until the day of making the banner, I hadn't realized how much this had affected me, and this moment became one of the first memories I have of being surrounded by people who shared my love for the same thing. It felt euphoric.

The night finally came. On 11 January 2012, the 1D T.E.A.M. arrived at the Hammersmith Apollo. We looked like a scene from *Mean Girls*, walking with our arms linked,

Jovilee Burton

wearing matching One Direction T-shirts, each personalized with our name. After an extended wait, which left us wondering if the boys were even going to bother turning up, a deafening scream erupted across the concert hall. I craned my neck to look at the stage and there they were. One Direction were on stage.

As I was singing along, my Miss Sporty mascara dripping down my face, I couldn't help but think how comfortable I felt in the crowd. I looked around at my fellow concertgoers, watching and studying them, noticing how the sensation I felt was identical to how I'd felt making the banner just days before. At random moments I'd hold my breath, trying to fully capture my surroundings. Young girls around me were full of glee, screaming, crying, belting out lyrics. Like me, they were in their element; we were all sharing a space together, our spirits in unison. When the music stopped and the audience sang the songs back to the band, it felt like a rallying cry. There I was, standing alongside people I'd never met and would never see again. But for those two hours, I was home. I felt at peace in a community of strangers. I was in a 'stranger community'.

After the concert, I became more obsessed with One Direction, going on Twitter and Tumblr incessantly, falling further into the rabbit hole. I found myself coming across other girls my age who loved One Direction as much as I did. We were an online community of fans, known by many as a 'fandom', and we called ourselves Directioners. Mainstream media painted us as obsessed, erratic tweens who were pathetically pining over five teenage boys. And that's exactly what we were! But at the time, I didn't see my fellow Directioners in this light. To me, they were family.

For the next few years, my presence in the Directioner community increased as I began to overcompensate for what I was lacking in real life. There was a reason why I craved online attention so much. My time in Essex was the same as that of most Black people raised in predominantly white areas: the growing pains associated with adolescence were peppered with the occasional microaggression, a sprinkle of overt racism and a dash of ignorance. Don't get me wrong: my friends were lovely and rarely malicious. But their niceness didn't protect me from the social seclusion I felt due to the colour of my skin, nor the racist utterances and jabs from those who were not in my circle. It didn't make up for the cultural differences our parents clearly exhibited. It didn't make me feel less alone.

I thought I was the problem, and, despite my best efforts to assimilate, my Blackness continued to be a marker of difference. I genuinely saw the colour of my skin as a source of shame. It destroyed my self-confidence during my formative years. There's a reason why films like *Get Out* resonate so much with Black people across the diaspora – we know what it's like to be an outsider in spaces that weren't built for us. No matter how well-meaning your peers may seem, it's always something that you're hyper-aware of. When I was in school, I could never shake it off, and this covert feeling of inferiority clung to me like my school jumper.

But on social media, the colour of my skin didn't matter. In the Directioner community, I was judged on one thing and one thing only: my love for the band. Since that had no bounds, I fitted right in and was able to find other girls my age online whose lives were as spectacularly dull as my own outside of their love for One Direction. I was opened up to a community that centred around a shared interest rather than identity markers. For a young girl in Essex, this was groundbreaking. The Directioner community was my escape. I wasn't the only Black girl in her friendship group, sheltered and lacking in self-confidence. I was Timi from @the_1D_team, the girl who'd occasionally go viral with her One Direction hot takes and who could recite the lyrics to every 1D single, B-side and album track off by heart. Finally, I had 24/7 access to a guaranteed circle of friends. Because I was no longer second-guessing what I wanted to say or stumbling over my words, I was able to find my voice. Through memes, Picnik photo edits and self-made GIFs, I found kinship in a world where I felt out of place.

I'm glad to say that as I got older I became more comfortable with and prouder of my Blackness. I no longer relied on the One Direction fandom to make me feel whole. (Also, Zayn, clearly the most beautiful band member, quit the group, so I got bored.) But, when looking back at my late teens and my time at university, I realize that some parts of twelve-year-old Timi never left. That stranger community I'd first experienced in Hammersmith Apollo in 2012 was something I continued to crave. I'd go to concerts, club nights, theatres – any event that had me surrounded by unfamiliar people. I'd establish two-hour-long relationships with strangers, feeling comfortable enough to share elements of myself with people I knew I'd never meet again, yet whom I instantly trusted because of our shared interest. I loved meeting other girls in the club toilets, chatting to my neighbour during the play intermission or leaning against the railings at a festival to converse with others while waiting for the act to come on stage.

For a lot of Black people, stranger communities act as a source of escapism from a world where we are routinely marginalized and ignored. Getting lost in the crowd at large-scale events or becoming immersed in online groups provides Black people with moments of joy so brief that they can sometimes be forgotten, yet are so important for long-term happiness. The BBC did a study in 2019 and found that developing brief connections with strangers every day can make life feel more pleasant. Humans are inherently social animals – that's why we find joy in live-tweeting *Drag Race* or *Love Island*, singing Burna Boy's 'Ye' in unison at the club, or doing the 'Candy' dance at every given opportunity.

Although stranger communities are not immune to the inequality and discrimination rampant in wider society, they can provide Black people with stability during years of deep insecurity and struggle as they come into their identity. It's normal to find comfort in stranger communities when you're feeling a bit lost in your own life – they act as a reminder that you never walk alone.

Black American artist and creator Aria Dean's work centres around the 'lonesome crowd', as she calls it, and the idea of being 'alone together'. She logs the presence of Black bodies in spaces through hip-hop music videos, recognizing how this medium sheds light on the power of the Black community, whose members empower each other and band together for support.

In an article for *gal-dem*, Nic Crosara also writes about the beauty of online spaces in fostering a sense of community and 'the magic of having a place to unapologetically be yourself even if only from behind a keyboard'. The article's conclusion personally resonated with me: 'I hope that . . . we will move beyond the idea that social media is objectively

"It's normal to find comfort in stranger communities when you're feeling a bit lost in your own life – they act as a reminder that you **never walk alone**" an unhealthy addiction (no matter how it is used) and move towards thinking of new ways to use technology to bring about mental well-being and community.' The impact of finding strangers online and offline cannot be ignored. Connecting with others who have similar lived experiences or shared interests naturally increases our sense of belonging.

For me, that feeling of being accepted by a group of strangers who are bound together by a common interest helped me in overcoming my mental health issues. The stranger community was there for me when my anxiety and depression were at an all-time high, providing support when I needed them most. I was raised in a Christian family and taught in church that homosexuality is a sin, and I knew that Christians close to me agreed with these teachings. During my late teens and early twenties, I began to come to terms with the fact that I wasn't straight. This revelation weighed me down, clouding my head with sadness and shame. No matter how much I dived into my stranger communities in the club and at concerts, in the back of my mind I felt guilty and worried that my family wouldn't accept me, or that my friends would judge me.

So, without realizing, I reverted back to my twelve-year-old ways, looking for new stranger communities who would understand me. After seeing LGBTQIA+ youth worker and influencer Tanya Compas talk at the 2018 Black Girl Fest, a yearly event in London for Black women and non-binary people, I followed her on Twitter and from there was introduced to the Black British queer community. Some people were like me and still in the closet; others were out and proud. But one thing was the same for all of us: we understood the specific experience of Black queer people in Britain. Like the Directioner fandom, this community provided me with a sense of belonging that I craved. I was able to explore my sexuality in a safe space and discuss topics I couldn't bring up with my friends and wouldn't dare share with my family. I thank the online Black queer community for giving me the confidence to show my true self to the world.

I came out to my parents in December 2020. It was terrifying and exhilarating, so much so that the whole experience remains quite foggy in my memory. Adrenaline was pumping through my veins. I had so much energy afterwards, and the only thing I could think of doing was rushing to Twitter to tell my followers the good news. As soon as I hit send, a wave of anxiety ran through me. Had I just opened myself up to online criticism? Was the Twitterverse going to hate me? I put my phone away, too scared to look. But after an hour of pacing around my room in fear, I checked my phone and was shocked. My notifications tab was full of positive messages, with strangers congratulating me for doing something so brave. People who didn't even follow me, or know who I was, were telling me how proud they were.

That euphoric feeling I'd got from the Hammersmith Apollo in 2012, from teenage girls on social media, from festivals and theatre halls, I experienced in my bedroom when I came out. Having strangers go out of their way to show care and support reminded me of the community I'd cherished as a tween from the fellow Directioners online. Stranger communities, whether online or offline, were so necessary for my life when I needed them the most and will continue to play an integral part in shaping the woman I grow up to be. For so many young Black Brits feeling isolated in their everyday life, these stranger communities remind us that we are worthy of love and respect. My stranger communities made me find out things about myself. They instilled in me a level of confidence that I would never have got anywhere else. They made me feel like me.

FIND YOUR OWN JOY

Get up a photo or video of the last live performance, club night or play you attended. Think back to how great it was getting lost in the crowd and feeling so free. What about it did you love?

" For so many young Black Brits feeling isolated in their everyday life, these stranger communities remind us that we are **worthy of love and respect** "

Homecoming

The intimacy
of meeting my
Jamaican family

Diane Abbott

POLITICIAN

One of the purest sources of Black joy for me has been being able to spend time in my parents' birthplace: the island nation of Jamaica. And my first ever visit was probably the most joyful. I was able to meet long-lost family, reconfigure how I find my peace in a white society and learn what the meaning of 'belonging' truly is.

I almost didn't make the trip. I was in my late teens and it was my mother's idea. She had suggested that we should visit together, and I unthinkingly said yes. After all, it would be a free holiday – what was not to like? But as the date of departure drew nearer, I decided that I could think of nothing more boring than going on holiday with my own mother, so I attempted to get out of it. That was when she revealed to me that her brothers in Jamaica had clubbed together to pay my plane fare. Unknown to me, they had heard of my achievements (no doubt lovingly recounted by my mother), which included grammar school and a place at Cambridge, and they wanted to see this young star for themselves. My mother insisted that I simply could not let them down. I was taken aback that people I didn't know and had never met cared enough about me to be determined to meet me. I had to go.

Even the literal journey there taught me things about love I didn't know before. My mother and father were very much part of the Windrush generation. They had been brought up in the same rural village: Smithville in the Jamaican parish of Clarendon. Their paths separated but they went on to travel to England around the same time. My father, whose adventurous streak I suspect I inherited, travelled by aeroplane; my mother took the more usual journey by boat to Southampton. But inevitably they met quite quickly, as the Jamaican community in London in the 1950s was extremely tight-knit. My father was walking down the street in Paddington one day when he met a cousin and close neighbour from Jamaica. She exclaimed at seeing him and told him that my mother was also in London. He went on to seek my mother out, one thing led to another and they married. Eventually the marriage collapsed and they went through a particularly acrimonious divorce, which resulted in my mother moving to Yorkshire.

At the time I firmly believed that their split was because of my father's tyrannical nature. Years later I realized that while my father was indeed an authoritarian who was a stranger to the tenets of women's liberation, much of his rage was about the things that he as a Black man was experiencing in white Britain half a century before there was any notion that Black lives mattered.

At the time of the trip to Jamaica, he and my mother were not speaking. But neither I nor my mother could drive and we needed a lift to the airport. I approached my father for the favour. A little to my surprise, he agreed. He turned up brooding and taciturn. As I remember, we drove in complete silence. But I will never forget walking through the busy airport alongside my father with all the suitcases piled on a luggage trolley as my mother walked behind. After a while, my father turned and looked at my mother struggling a little to keep up. He said softly, in his distinctive Jamaican accent, 'She did always walk slow.' It was just a sentence. But with that one remark, I realized that he had loved my mother since they were schoolchildren in rural Jamaica and that he loved her still.

When we landed in Jamaica, I had no idea what to expect. We began by staying with my mother's sister in the lower-middle-class district of Duhaney Park in Kingston, the capital city. It was not the tourists' Jamaica. There was no beach, no palm trees and no limbo dancers – none of the visual clichés that British people associate with the Caribbean. This part of Kingston consisted of rows of little owner-occupied houses. My aunt used to refer to them as 'Mr Matalon's matchboxes', in reference to the Jamaican developer who built them. My aunt was immensely proud of her spotless little house, which had been purchased by her daughter with money earned working overseas as a teacher.

Although it was all relatively mundane, there was still much to marvel at. I had known my aunt in London, but now that she had retired and gone home to Jamaica she looked remarkably happy and healthy. And the quality of the light, even in urban Kingston, was very different from grey London. The streetscapes and the easy way people carried themselves enchanted me. My aunt went out of her way to be hospitable, the food was delicious, and the idea that I was somewhere that I had, unwittingly, known all my life tugged at my emotions.

In a way, I *had* known the country all my life. When I was growing up in London, my parents would regularly meet up with Jamaican friends and family to reminisce about 'home'. The Jamaican places they talked about repeatedly, such as May Pen, Frankfield and Half Way Tree, were as familiar to me as Shepherd's Bush, Portobello Road, Piccadilly Circus and Middlesex. The one thing that couldn't be conveyed through place names alone was the sheer beauty of the island. I have travelled all over the world since I first visited Jamaica, but it remains, for me, one of the most beautiful places in the world. And although I like a beach as much as the next person, personally I find the real beauty of Jamaica to be in its beautiful green countryside.

My journey to visit the country where my parents were born is one that many young Black British people have experienced. It is almost a rite of passage, a Windrush-style trek in reverse to try to understand your roots, especially if you are a descendant of the enslaved. To an extent, your perceptions before you visit may have been framed by the fact that you have been raised in a white society where the mainstream media trades in stereotypes. This means that when you arrive in your ancestral home, you'll probably be in for a surprise. Not everyone finds the same sense of belonging as I did in Jamaica, but the emotions it raises for you, as a Black person likely entering a predominantly Black country for the first time, will be profound.

Some people, especially Black Caribbean Brits who haven't visited for many years, might be surprised to hear me speak so positively about Jamaica. Thanks in part to the British media, there has been a picture painted of the island that is not entirely accurate. While, yes, there are areas that are more dangerous than others – as is the case in any country – Jamaica is not just the sun, sea and sand clichés. It is a country that sits proudly in its history, which has developed its own magnificent postcolonial culture and exported it to the world through food, music and dance. It has its problems, sure, but I have only felt love when I have visited. Especially on my first trip, that embrace held me tight.

The highlight of that first visit was my mother and I going to spend time with my grandmother, Miss Di. She still lived in the tiny rural village that my mother and her siblings had been brought up in. Smithville is on a crossroads in the heart of the Jamaican countryside, with the green hills of Clarendon on every side. Those hills were significant, not just because they were so lovely but because this was where many formerly enslaved people fled after abolition when they refused to cut sugar cane for the white man any more. Instead, they chose to scratch a living in the hills, growing coffee and enough food for their families. They were poor, but they were free. This produced a certain boldness and independence of spirit which I think you can detect in the descendants of rural Jamaicans wherever you find them in the world.

My grandmother herself, who I was meeting for the first time, was in her sixties and had an easy grace and dignity. Over the years, in common with so many of their generation of Jamaicans, most of her children had travelled to Britain and North America for work. For Jamaican immigrant families to survive in those times, there was no question of women staying home to look after children and they often sent them back to their mothers in Jamaica to be looked after. My family was the same. But I was the grandchild that Miss Di had not brought up, so I was a marvel to her. We had a lovely visit. I remember her little house, which had no electricity and was lit by oil lamps, and an outhouse where she cooked and stored food.

Eventually, we had to leave. My mother and I had travelled to Smithville from Kingston on a country bus, and we had to return by it too. This was an adventure and a uniquely Jamaican experience in itself. My grandmother insisted on helping us with our luggage. I was a little surprised to realize that what she meant by that was piling all our suitcases on top of her head. I will never forget the sight of her by the roadside waiting with us for the bus. She was serene, exquisitely lovely and ramrod straight. In future years, whenever I had to do something that I was nervous about, perhaps speaking at a public event, to give myself courage I would remember that particular image of my grandmother: fearless and proud.

Another wonderful visit on that first trip to Jamaica was going to see my mother's favourite brother, Uncle Len. He lived in the suburbs of Kingston, up on the hillside in an area called Stony Hill. This was a grander part of Kingston than Duhaney Park, and my uncle had a beautiful house with a swimming pool. He was an extremely dignified, dark-skinned man. A bachelor, he had invested his salary in land and property. He loved native Jamaican art and sculpture, and his own house was full of carefully curated artworks, which he introduced me to. I spent many evenings by the swimming pool at Uncle Len's house, surrounded by green hills, eating exquisite Jamaican meals and chatting. He loved to talk.

Even though initially I wasn't sure that I wanted to visit Jamaica at all, I would go on to return year after year and to spend time with Uncle Len. I would ring him from

London explaining that I was thinking of coming to stay on a particular date and he would say firmly, 'Just come.' My room was always ready and there was always a welcome rum punch. What was fascinating about Uncle Len was that he led such a stylish, but very culturally Jamaican, life. He had recently retired from an administrative job with the telephone company Cable & Wireless, which was a major employer on the island. Uncle Len never complained, but as I got to know him over the years I realized that many career avenues would have been barred to him because, in a highly colour-conscious colonial Jamaica, he would have been deemed 'too dark'. In some ways, his job at Cable & Wireless was an acme of achievement.

Over the years, he related many anecdotes and explained to me the history of my family, unravelling the interlocking web of cousins and, very importantly, setting out who was a real uncle or aunt and who was just a very close neighbour. I had many relatives in Jamaica, but Uncle Len was the one that I felt closest to. He always longed to come and visit my mother in England, but sadly died before that was possible.

The main thing that has always made visiting Jamaica so joyful for me and cemented the feeling of belonging is the personal affirmation of basking in unconditional love from family and friends, which works as a healing balm when, as a Black woman in Britain, you experience so many racial macro- and microaggressions from white society. Jamaican passengers habitually clap when their plane touches down on the island. When I first heard them do this, I thought it was a tribute to the skills of the pilot. But after my first few flights I realized that they were expressing their intense relief and delight at being away from the endless racial microaggressions that characterize the Black experience in Britain.

Growing up in the UK, I had to survive in a series of all-white institutions – first my grammar school, and then Cambridge and the House of Commons. Even the part of London I grew up in, Harrow, was virtually all white when I was a child. One of the first things that I realized on visiting Jamaica was just how much pressure I was under in England. I experienced the amazing feeling of the stress from all those racial microaggressions, exacerbated in recent years by the rise of online platforms such as Twitter (which have made it all too easy for people to spew abuse, venom and racial hatred into your personal space), rolling off my shoulders. They can be so routine that you become almost desensitized to them. One of my mottos has always been that I refuse to make white people's problems my own, but it's much easier when you are removed from their structures.

From that very first visit, Jamaica has given me strength that has persisted throughout my adult life. At some of the worst times in my life, Jamaica is where I have fled to in order to heal. But above all, as a country that speaks to my culture, my family and my ancestry, it has given me joy through a deep sense of belonging.

FIND YOUR OWN JOY

Pour yourself a rum and Coke, or your favourite drink that reminds you of wherever you call home.

" Jamaica is where
I have fled to in order
to heal. But above all,
as a country that
speaks to my
culture, my family
and my ancestry,
**it has given me
joy through a deep
sense of belonging** "

First Kiss

How I make space for remembering love

Fopé Ajanaku

WRITER & YOUTH WORKER

I want to tell you about joy and pleasure. Are you sitting comfortably?

> *I wanted it to be you.*
> *I wanted it to be you so badly.*

Kathleen Kelly, *You've Got Mail*

They kissed and my tiny heart exploded.

I think about kissing a lot. In the abstract sense, being close enough to someone to bestow a kiss is a fantasy I held on to with clenched fingers throughout lockdown. But, if I'm honest, I think about kissing in a very real and horny sense a lot more. Feeling the sweat of someone's upper lip against yours, the clack of your teeth before you readjust into a smooth glide. Clammy hands tensing against your waist, relaxing if only for a moment to grip you closer when you press into them. The wet squelch of your tongues, and a fleshy bottom lip held between your canines. It's intoxicating in a way that I cannot fully describe. I constantly daydream about grabbing someone's head closer to mine, the shorter hairs on the nape of their neck tucked away in my fingers. In movies, the orchestral accompaniment swells at a good finale kiss, but in my good and earnest opinion it will always pale in comparison to the real thing: the rhythm of their moans working in tandem with yours as you try to climb into each other, the percussion of your gasps leaving your lips in staccato bursts. A whispered plea, once, twice. You are a god and they are your supplicant. Praise and worship has never sounded so good – no film soundtrack can beat that.

Are you thinking about kissing? Did you pause to take a breath?

Good.

We don't get to pause and think about love a lot, do we? As the eldest child of a single Black mother, there was never enough time. There's always something to do. There's always more surviving to do. We'll think of love when we get there. My mum used to say, 'That's life, and life isn't fair,' whenever I complained, and it would infuriate me no end. Why can't we spend eternity trapped bathing in what makes us feel alive?

Being in love is being in cahoots: the conspiring activity of people up to no good. It's the best ploy or narrative device of them all, and only you and I are in on it. Don't you love a secret? (Don't you love a ruse?) You can create whole galaxies within a kiss, unearthed languages within a touch, and a shared ancient codex with your eyes. It is the best thing we have to offer in this bleak and quickly decaying society we call the present. Black people have refused to let go of love and clung on to it desperately throughout our entire history. I always think of the fact that even when enslaved, our ancestors still

"Black people have refused to let go of love and clung on to it desperately throughout our entire history**"**

had wedding ceremonies. Imagine that. The ceremonies were small and had no legal standing (since enslaved people were denied citizenship or the right of marriage), but they were soaked with tradition carried over oceans. The world right now feels as if it is getting older and meaner and harsher, and as Black people sometimes we need to remind ourselves of, to quote the indomitable Céline Dion, *the power of love*.

For as long as I can remember, I have been obsessed with the fantasy of love in all its manifestations. Films, books, TV shows – you name it, I have been there. Both tangible and immaterial, yet incredibly elusive, love is something I have spent the better part of my life sniffing out wherever and whenever I can. I yearned to be like the movie heroines, to have weak knees and be silly and giddy and in love.

It all started with one film. I remember clutching a beaded pillow to my chest when Nora Ephron's Shopgirl (Meg Ryan) and NY152 (Tom Hanks) in *You've Got Mail* (1988) revealed themselves to one another and *finally* kissed. Meg Ryan's tearful *I wanted it to be you. I wanted it to be you so badly* and that perfect pale blue dress and matching cardigan have lived on the top floor of my mind for over two decades now. They hold my heart entirely.

Even as my mother did my hair and held steadfast control of the remote, amid the yanking of my roots and the continuous reprimand of 'Face that way!', I would still find ways to sneak peeks at the Nollywood film she had stuck on. Despite the chaos, those films felt familiar to me in a way that Hollywood never did. Famous 2000s Nigerian actresses such as Genevieve Nnaji, Ini Edo and Omotola Jalade Ekeinde were my starlets of the green-and-white screen, existing perfectly separately to the stars of Hollywood, and they looked just like me. We had a mountain of copied DVDs leaning precariously against the PC, and once a week I was allowed to choose one. Sordid tales of adultery, dubious morals and the power of love conquering everything under the banner of puritanical West African Christianity were my bread and butter throughout my adolescence. I mean, what is faith if not love sustained?

I came here tonight because when you realize you want to spend the rest of your life with somebody, you want the rest of your life to start as soon as possible.

Harry Burns, *When Harry Met Sally*

The first time I really conceptualized what love was and what it meant to me was in a middling primary school in southeast London, when I was utterly and miserably in love with my best friend. His name was Daniel. Our mums always said hello to each other at the school gates. His laugh made my belly flutter before I knew what butterflies were.

I still remember the day I told him I *like* liked him, mainly because that level of embarrassment is hard to forget. It's amazing what you can tell from the slight twitch of a hand, the small pause before they reply and the beginnings of a frown. In a millisecond I had my answer, but I still had to endure the excruciating five minutes and subsequent weeks of ritual humiliation that followed my first ever rejection.

'I'm sorry – I've only ever seen you as a friend.'

(By lunchtime everyone knew.)

Friend.

Unsurprisingly, this wasn't the only rejection I faced. I was seventeen in Delphi, Greece, on a school trip and drunker than I had been in my entire life thus far. I'm watching the most beautiful girl in my year slowly grind with someone else to 'Timber' by Kesha featuring Pitbull. I am miserably in love and I think we're meant to be. I watch as her hand curves past the swell of an arse and comes to rest on the sweaty peekaboo of a back. In a moment of true recklessness, obviously encouraged by three consecutive shots of tequila that definitely should not have been sold to me, I tell her.

We're standing opposite one another on a funny little cobbled street, straight out of a storybook. The air is warm and balmy, and my hands are wet and sticky. I tell her how her name is tattooed on my heart. I tell her of my jealousy.

I tell her that I love her.

'Oh, I thought we were just friends?'

(I try to play it off, but our friendship is never the same.)

Friends.

Remember in school, in the autumn, when all the boys would shake the chestnut trees and conkers would rain down on our heads as we screamed with laughter, and someone would always jump high into the air to crush one underneath their boots? Do you remember that sound? The crack that pierced the air? I like to think that's what my heart sounded like in that playground and in that street in that tiny little town in Greece. Like a conker, splitting right down the middle.

> *Heartbreak opens on to the sunrise*
> *For even breaking is opening*
> *And I am broken*
> *I am open*
> *Broken to the new light without pushing in*
> *Open to the possibilities within, pushing out*
> *See the love shine in through my cracks*
> *See the light shine out through me?*
> *I am broken*
> *I am open*
> *I am broken open*

See the love light shining through me
Shining through my cracks
Through the gaps
My spirit takes journey
My spirit takes flight
Could not have risen otherwise
And I am not running
I am choosing
Running is not a choice
From the breaking
Breaking is freeing
Broken is freedom
I am not broken
I am free.

Alike, *Pariah*

I broke up with my first proper boyfriend over the phone. This was a turbulent and short-lived relationship in my second year of university, filled with slamming doors and screaming matches at least once a week. On that last ever phone call, I sat anxiously perched on the edge of the bed, like a bird getting ready to take flight. 'This isn't love, is it? This can't be it, because I'm never happy. Are you?' Looking back, I was so sure that if I explained it reasonably and logically, he would understand and we would part ways as great friends. Instead, he told me he lied the first time he said he loved me; he told me I was broken; he told me that I wasn't made to be loved.

I remember hearing the roar of a plane cruise across the sky through the open window, followed by the jarring buzzing of the downstairs entranceway as I cried fat, loud and ugly tears down the phone to a boy I was so sure was the love of my life five seconds prior. It's weird, isn't it? How certain memories will always stick with us? I couldn't now tell you his surname or recount the way his lips felt on mine.

But I still remember the cruel twist of his words. I still remember thinking, 'Oh, *this* is heartbreak. This is what it feels like to be dying over and over again in the same second. This is what they meant.'

I adore films because even the open endings are still that: endings. But there was no ending here – just vicious words, a lot of tears, years of therapy and then . . . nothing. I am not the main character; he is not the villain. There is no divine justice. There is just the rubble left in the remnants of our hearts and the weapons they choose to bludgeon you with.

In my darkest moments of heartbreak, when my heart is numb and my eyes are dull, I wonder whether it's worth it. I know you're thinking about it now. The tumultuous winds of love have battered my sails time and time again, and each time I ask myself, 'How can a feeling armed with razor-sharp teeth ever bring you joy?'

> *But I know about suffering; if that helps.*
> *I know that it ends. I ain't going to tell you no*
> *lies, like it always ends for the better. Sometimes*
> *it ends for the worse. You can suffer so bad that*
> *you can be driven to a place where you can't*
> *ever suffer again: and that's worse.*

Sharon Rivers, *If Beale Street Could Talk*

I found freedom in an orgasm.

('Is this still an essay about love?')

('Yes. Desire is important, right? It's the foundation of our attraction, the kernel that grows into love. Maybe. Keep reading.')

I have grown to love hotel rooms and the emotional implications the empty rooms come with. I wonder if the memories of every body that has slid under the same crisp white sheets imprints on you. They are both neutral ground and a space to the left of reality, where anything can happen. It's there I found sex to be freeing and truly pleasurable, without the limitations of a curfew or the imposition of a car pulling into the drive.

We undressed one another with none of the coyness of new lovers. His arms gripped me so tight I thought I would combust. I gasped in surprise as we fell on to the bed, like it hadn't occurred to me until just that moment that this was something we were going to do. The heavens didn't split open and the earth didn't shake to pieces under me, but by the end I was breathing hard and fast, satisfied in a way I felt right down to the base of my spine.

Older and not a bit wiser, I care less about the explosive nature of love, less about the dramatic confessions and the big collisions that define our lives. The moments the films don't show you intrigue me far more. Those moments that you forget about – not because they are forgettable but because they are mundane in a sort of precious way. When I look back at these small, loosely unfurled moments (memories that make you squeeze your legs tightly together and stop in the middle of a sentence), my heart swells with warmth and fondness. This is where I always fall in love.

It's the shared shower the morning after. It's when falling naked into bed feels intimate but somehow not sexual. When all conversations feel like a well-worn slipper, shared only between the two of you. When they say your name in the exact same way they whisper *fuck* in bed.

His head is lying on my naked chest and he is curled around me. We are so close to one another that I know that if I move I will have to slowly peel my skin off his. Yet he pulls me closer. I am smiling so hard my jaw will ache for days to come.

Sometimes as I lie in my bed all alone, I stretch and reach out to the farthest points in my room. I miss the feeling of tangling my toes with someone else's. That shock of cold as they find warmth among mine. I miss the particular smell of when someone sleeps next to you. I miss grazing a soft belly with the back of my hand and hearing a sleepy rendition of my name escape their lips.

Sometimes I imagine it's you.

You loved on my neck hard and left a mark the size of a 50p coin behind. It was dark and red and angry, and I spent the rest of the day ridiculing you for secondary-school behaviour on my Instagram story. *Can you believe this nerd?* I captioned a risqué photo of my neck erring on the side of inappropriate, with a hint of my nipple peeking through the bottom left corner. But when I was in the bathroom later, standing naked and alone, I stared in the mirror at that mark, pressed my fingers hard on the bruise and thought, *Oh. Oh. This is what they meant. This is how your heart fills up. How can it not be worth the pain?*

Romance is about the possibility of the thing.
You see, it's about the time between when you

first meet the woman, and when you first make
love to her. When you first ask a woman to
marry you, and when she says, 'I do.' When
people who've been together a long time say
that the romance is gone, what they're really
saying is they've exhausted the possibility.

Darius Lovehall, *Love Jones*

The pale dawn sunlight filters through my window. There is no one in my unmade bed, and there are no eyes watching the straps of my camisole slowly slide down my shoulder as I write. It seemed a romantic notion at the time, thinking about love through the films that made me. But as a flame the size of my fingernail flickers in the cold night air rolling into my bedroom, I can't help but feel like I'm waiting for someone, my scene partner, to fill the silence with their scripted flirting, a dynamic foil to my role as the protagonist.

Sometimes I do have to ask, however, how do you still centre love, still have the energy to *yearn*, when life is telling you that it's not yours to keep? At some point, choosing to love and be loved despite the pain it may bring is a radical choice. It's a decision we make every day, to choose to go forward. As a child, I desperately wanted to hold love to my chest with my grubby little fingers and never let it out of my grasp. Today I still cling, but in truth my arms have grown weary.

I watched these films because they filled me with a sense of wonder. We live such long lives on this blue ball floating through the cosmos, and in a world where traditional norms that catered to the unbearable whiteness of being want us to feel isolated, to feel that we as Black people are unworthy and undeserving of love, I have come to realize that we owe it to ourselves to remain just as in love with the idea of love as being in love. To over-romanticize, to dream too big and to hope for too much. You are allowed to mull over the most miniscule of moments. To let that text exchange stay in your mind months after the fact.

10:04

for what it's worth, i will always love u

10:05

for what it's worth, same

The American philosopher Dr Joy James once said: 'Love should be our right and the longevity of love is our birthright.' I believe that. Do you?

Do you remember your first kiss? Do you remember that feeling of being held? Mine was stunning and gorgeous and I was sweaty and nervous and all I could think as they pressed me into my locker and as my heart bloomed was: *It's happening, holy fuck it's happening.*

This is what they were talking about. This was the joy they spoke of.

FIND YOUR OWN JOY

Pour yourself a glass of your favourite drink and cook yourself a hearty meal. (Alternatively, order a takeaway – the result is the same. You will be fed.)

CHARACTERS' LINES HAVE BEEN QUOTED FROM THE FOLLOWING:
Pariah: screenplay by Dee Rees, directed by Dee Rees (Chicken and Egg Pictures/MBK Entertainment/Northstar Pictures/Pariah Feature/Sundial Pictures/aid+abet, 2011)
You've Got Mail: screenplay by Nora Ephron and Delia Ephron (based on the play *Parfumerie* by Miklós László), directed by Nora Ephron (Lauren Shuler Donner Productions/Warner Bros, 1998)
When Harry Met Sally: screenplay by Nora Ephron, directed by Rob Reiner (Castle Rock Entertainment/Nelson Entertainment, 1989)
If Beale Street Could Talk: written by James Baldwin (Dial Press, 1964)
Love Jones: screenplay by Theodore Witcher, directed by Theodore Witcher (Addis Wechsler Pictures, 1997)

A
Photograph
The beauty
in the mundane
experience

Bukky Bakray

ARTIST & ACTOR

Illustration by Tomekah George

One summer night, a while back, I was sitting on the steps outside my friend's house, talking about the downsides of life, when a Black family of six walked past. Laughing and hugging, they were clearly enjoying each other's company. They meandered down the road confidently, as though it was their forefathers who built it. I remember one of the men was in a crisp white T-shirt, the other dressed in black. One of the women had brown locs with grey highlights that almost seemed to float in the air. Another wore a see-through blouse made from a delicately patterned fabric. Their exposed skin was glistening, and when they smiled the brightness of their teeth reflected off the street lamps.

In *Notes of a Native Son*, James Baldwin wrote that 'experience is a private, very largely speechless affair'. When I saw this family, my speech was stolen. In that moment, I felt how I normally feel when I watch a film by Barry Jenkins: transfixed by a narrative other than my own. And that narrative was soft and subtle. As I sat there, beginning to get lost in this family's joy, I saw artistry. A portrait that didn't need shine or embellishment. A moment, if painted, that would make people question what the word 'masterpiece' means. I often wish I had captured it in 35mm film, so I could hold on to it forever, look back on it as a tangible memory and give it a nostalgic tone. I am in love with elements of 'the past' that it feels celestial.

Tomekah George

For a long time before this, I had thought deeply about how marginal Black people appear in this universe. This scene was a counter-narrative to years of often negative and repetitive depictions. Since then, I have captured more gripping moments of Black people like this one and kept them in my sea of memories. I promise you I am not an oddity. I just cannot help but obsess over the true beauty and actuality of the mundane Black experience. I have discovered that much of my joy can be found in the moments where I have not sought permission nor asked for it, but rather taken and protected it. With delightful rebellion, moments of ordinary, un-bedazzled, beautiful mundanity have become my resistance, my activism.

It is the link-ups with a handful of friends, the spontaneous meetings that turn into endless nights; it is the sit-ins where we watch films and TV all day. The dinners. The walks home from secondary school. Listening to hip-hop and soul albums from start to finish, feeling like electricity. The unaccompanied stroll taking in the street sounds, thinking of nothing in particular. The 50p given to you as a child that would take you to Malta, the Maldives, the Caribbean and even some parts of West Africa where you would sip cocktails when you were thirsty (translation: running out your house to the street ahead, where your neighbours were waiting to play, then sipping on fruity canned drinks and slush puppies that you bought from the nearby corner shop).

Some of my favourite memories are of getting food with my friends and just chilling and eating. We would go to the same chicken shop and talk about the same problems every single day. It was mundane, but we were satisfied. Now we all have money and are vegan, so we don't set foot inside. I don't miss the pigeon meat, but I deeply miss the memories that came with it. Even the lonesome days of my adolescence, when I clung to music by artists with similar identities to me, were special. For some people, like myself, simple moments act as ingredients in the recipe for joy.

I have spent much of my life chasing contentment. It often appears close, only to dissolve into nothingness once in reach. The heat of my Black skin simultaneously creates the beauty I see in the world and destroys it. Because, while being Black is wonderful, it is also a complex phenomenon. It is to be everything to everyone: to fight, but not be animalistic; to be passionate, but not too much; to protest, but not too loudly; to stand tall, but not intimidate. And, finally, to be a spokesperson or proxy for political motives as opposed to simply being an individual. I often wonder what I would make of the world if I hadn't been forced to ascribe to the boundaries of race.

" For some people, like myself, simple moments act as **ingredients in the recipe for joy** "

The philosopher Frantz Fanon spoke in a relatable way on how he saw himself as a Black man in a white context in a 1952 essay titled 'The Fact of Blackness': 'I subjected myself to an objective examination, I discovered my blackness, my ethnic characteristics; and I was battered down by tom-toms, cannibalism, intellectual deficiency, fetishism, racial defects, slave-ships, and above all else, above all: "Sho' good eatin".' This quote both encapsulates my point and makes me laugh because it reminds me of how disrupted our experience is by anti-Blackness.

Because of our history, I sometimes feel it would be silly, maybe even unfair, to spend my evenings watching a film like Steve McQueen's *Lovers Rock* – about a house party in 1980, where Black characters sing along to reggae, gyrate, dance, sweat, kiss, celebrate, overcome and drown in joy – when, only a few clicks away, a documentary on the disproportionate representation of Black people in prison awaits. How can I find the time for love stories set in 1970s Harlem when the reading lists examining the impact of social justice movements grow daily? In some ways, I feel it would be reductive to engage in conversations that have no political links or themes when there are responsibilities to bear and conversations to carry.

But then I remember that the fight against racism should not be the entirety of anyone's existence.

*

When I saw that Black family drift past me, it made me suddenly emotional because it looked like something I had never seen depicted before but had always felt. We often forget how much life is led by what we see and what we consume. I see words and experiences; I see what the world allows me to see. In that moment, I realized that the scope of my Black British experience was dual, and often in conflict. I knew what I felt – the love of my friends and family and my community – but I rarely saw it depicted in such a day-to-day way. Walking quietly into the everyday lives of people you will never be, like that Black family, makes you appreciate your own experiences and long for better ones.

As a creator, visual imagery is special to me. When I started acting, the whole idea of seeing myself on-screen seemed really abstract. It's not quite the same as holding a mirror up to yourself. It's more a sense of undeniable recollection and identification. Like *feeling* yourself on-screen as opposed to seeing. The camera changes the ways in which we see experiences in motion. Being able to capture moments visually makes way for escapism, especially in films that act as a reminder of the beauty in the mundane.

This is why films like *Rocks*, *Moonlight*, *If Beale Street Could Talk* and *The Last Tree* are so essential. Millions of dollars were invested into the portrayal of arguably unremarkable lives that Black people can identify with. As Barry Jenkins himself explained during an interview with *Vice*: 'I think it's really important to remind [. . .] people that their lives have value, you know? That their lives have worth.' His storytelling reminded me of the value in my own life. As much as I appreciate films that transcend gender, race and class by launching Black people into alternate universes, like *Black Panther*, film-makers like Jenkins, Ikoko and Wilson help us fall back in love with the world as it is. We should never forget the depth of reality and the joy that can be found there.

Another huge part of my experience has been the joy I've felt within my real-life relationships. When I look around at my peers, I feel that we all have deep-rooted connections – not only through our Blackness but just as people. My schooldays with my forever friends were always punctuated with laughter. We used to laugh about the same things for years every single day – the epitome of mundane but absolutely foundational to who I have become. I am blessed because I have been surrounded by so many people who have opened the door for me to my own temple.

Before I started acting, I couldn't really look people in the eye because it felt too intimate. One of the writers of *Rocks*,

Theresa Ikoko, saw me and said that I couldn't talk to her unless I could meet her eyes. I wasn't going to miss out on the experience of being in conversation with her, so I just started to use eye contact a little more. Now I'm running around quoting playwrights saying the eyes are the windows to the soul. The memory of my head physically elevating, having to look up at people, shows me how these encounters changed me. I don't know if it's fair to call this a mundane experience, but the circumstance of the conversation between us was. We were just sitting in a cafe in London drinking hot chocolate. The scenery wasn't as elaborate as a Mayfair restaurant, but who would have known that would be a life-shifting moment?

*

Sometimes I have looked up at the sky and been in great envy of the stars: their beauty and the way they glisten, the community they have among other stars. The simplicity of their existence and how peaceful they look. How they manage to light up the sky together, side by side in unison. How no one would dare to question or interrupt their existence. There is an obvious dissimilarity between the stars' existence and my own. And although I am envious and long for a similar experience, I am grateful for the one that I have. The stars seem so mundane, uncomplicated and not intensely important, but are actually far from that. This notion makes me think that these mundane experiences that we have are incredibly misunderstood and more intricate than we could ever imagine.

Throughout my life I have not been able to avoid seeing quotes about how the ancestors did not fall for us to be so small. But what if they did? Years ago, my ancestors had moments of joy among themselves, despite colonial paradigms making us believe that our people were not cultured until they lived in another context. In Nigeria, Yoruba people were dancing way before colonizers played their tunes. Being a part of the Nigerian diaspora, I don't know much about my ancestors, but I do know they enjoyed vivid cuisines, shared stories and listened to the sounds released from their tongues. Day and night. They lived ordinarily and imperfectly.

There are times when I think of the end of it all and I drift into an image of myself sitting on a large dinner table drinking wine I can't pronounce, with plates of pork chops sweating with pig grease, jellies, steak flambés, filets mignons and caviar on the side, sitting beside people I don't even know. But I smile, throw out a few artificial laughs and talk about my thoughts and feelings on current affairs and Greenpeace. You see, the thing about nightmares is that sometimes they're even clearer than dreams. This nightmare is of a future me, who escaped the mundane and entered an exceptional lifestyle my soul couldn't take. One full of huge things, glamorous, unnecessary things that don't actually bring me happiness.

The little experience I have has taught me a lot of things and one of the most important is to eradicate size and amount unless we are talking about food. Thinking of largeness ruins everything. My experience is made up of many ingredients. I think it's much more fitting to take and live depending on how you feel not what you're meant to feel. I know what chilling with friends, family and God does to my body as opposed to being in a room with household names or being a household name. I'd rather just 'be' in my household.

*

When I think back to the mundanity of that Black family that drifted past me, I think of my own family, my soul sisters and brothers especially (the Black Sopranos). I think of the colour palettes, garments and sceneries in my own experiences and I hold on to them. Beside those memories are the ancestral histories, albums, diets, teachings and things that might literally mean nothing to others but so much to someone else. My Black British experience is far from a linear one, as I am honestly still a baby who is learning and existing. But to reiterate again: I am blessed and always grateful.

This life can be difficult and sad – that's inevitable – but there are some really beautiful parts that can be sought out. In my case they're mundane, but for some they may be extraordinary. That's cool, as long as we're honest about what we want. It's nice to be able to hold on to the simpler parts of life, which often get forgotten. Notice the things you often overlook, the colour of the sky, the sound of your friend's laugh, the way the trees grow, the people walking down a quiet street. Beauty in the mundane, everyday experience is ours to find.

FIND YOUR OWN JOY

Go outside or look out of your window. Stare at the sky and breathe for a couple of seconds. Live life in motion.

"Beauty in the everyday Black experience is ours to find **"**

Removing the Mask

Rethinking my masculinity to honour my inner child

Richie Brave
PRESENTER, WRITER & BROADCASTER

WARNING: this essay discusses suicidal thoughts and feelings which some readers may find upsetting or triggering.

I'll be honest. Growing up, my joy was often skewed by a restrictive idea of masculinity and a disconnect from the beauty of it that left me feeling suffocated. In honour of that, these words aren't just what I think you deserve but what a younger me needed to hear to connect to the joy within himself.

It would be better for me to give you a real insight into part of my journey rather than bullshit you with what I think you want to read. I want you to relax, unclench your jaw and loosen your shoulders while you read this. I want you to understand that joy is an individual, ever-changing journey as opposed to a pre-defined destination. You do not *have* to be the version of it you see online if you don't want to be. There is no one way for Black men to be joyful. You do not need to be perfect and you do not have to be sure. Joy is purest when you are able to be your complete self. I want to tell you how I truly embraced masculinity and a sense of joy that allowed me to love every part of me.

I'll move past the joy that came with the innocence of early childhood and say that seventeen was the age I experienced true joy for the first time – though all the while I was hyper aware of myself emerging from the hazy veil of early youth.

My teenage years up until that point were extremely difficult socially: I wasn't cool enough, handsome enough, talented enough, masculine enough or hard enough, and

" There is no one way for Black men to be joyful. You do not need to be perfect and you do not have to be sure. **Joy is purest when you are able to be your complete self** " that resulted in social rejection and, at times, unspeakable violence. To the best of my recollection, I was jumped five times as a boy. Some of those times I was set up by people who were meant to be my friends. I need people to understand the actuality of having your head stamped on, being punched and having knives drawn on you because the essence of who you are doesn't give you enough social capital – this was my reality. I was (and still am) emotional, gentle and caring, which, for the environment I described, made me a target. My teenage self went about building walls to counteract that. It left me mildly protected but constantly misunderstood.

I see the gentler qualities as strengths now, but back then I lived behind the same mask that so many Black boys and men have to wear and one that many people do not bother to lift and look under. It's a mask that disconnects us from who we are and, just as importantly, disconnects us from each other. I think about that in relation to the other Black boys I grew up around, even the ones I fought: how much of that conflict was about whatever we were protecting ourselves from or projecting, and how different it could have been if we'd chosen to see the softness in each other. That's how I feel when I think about Black Boy Joy specifically – not just the concept of embracing one's own true happiness but how we provide space for others to embody that for themselves.

My late teens did not start off easy: I was spiralling following the murder of my cousin, whom I was *very* close to, and I began to lose myself in grief. But during that time I was attending a weekend performing arts school and started to hang around with a group of people who changed my life forever. There were four of us as a core group – three boys, one girl – and others who frequently joined the fold. We were a group of working-class Black teenagers growing up in London, with all the joys and pains that come with that. We were unsure and finding ourselves, and I think we silently saw that in each other and held on. This is why I have an issue with people throwing around the term 'trauma bonding' with no context. My younger self needed a space to sort through my feelings, and our friendship group needed each other's love in the purest sense. I often hear people say you shouldn't look for your joy in others, but I would challenge this by saying sometimes it takes another person, or several people, to wake up the joy you have inside yourself. They did that for me. I am welling up in happiness writing this because at that point in my life I was low and used to spend hours in my room overcome with grief, considering suicide but never telling a soul. I was empty. I've never had the opportunity to tell my chosen family how they saved my life. I am glad I am sharing it now, with them and with you.

We bonded quickly and spent two years in a whirlwind of

constant laughter; I remember the pain of losing my cousin being offset by the escapism and unbridled happiness that came with being part of a group that loved me relentlessly. I think back to summers spent speaking until the sun came up and only going home to shower before we met each other again later in the day. I think about going to parties together, doing stupid dances in sync in the middle of the dance floor and taking over the room within minutes. I think of the looks of admiration from others seeing the bond between us. I remember sharing secrets and jokes in the early hours of the morning in hushed tones so we wouldn't wake our parents. I remember piling on to one bed together and falling asleep from the sheer exhaustion of being out and enjoying ourselves. I think of being hugged and told I was loved by a male friend for the first time. I think about late-night trips to McDonald's. I think about nicknames like Wizzy, 1-4, Gambit and Richie CUT (which they still refer to me as now, even in my thirties). I remember being held as I cried. I remember dancing until my feet hurt. I remember being huddled in small cars. I remember rap battles. I remember playful banter that never hit below the belt. I remember laughing until I couldn't breathe. I remember us supporting one of the group through depression. I remember vulnerability. I remember love.

They taught me how to be carefree while being *careful* with others' feelings and my own. I learned what it was like to trust someone outside of my family and it was the first time in my life where I didn't feel like I needed to be anyone but myself; I was accepted in my entirety. As soon as I was around them, I forgot about my mask. I forgot about the hurtful, toxic friendships of my mid-teens. I knew what it was like to feel safe. I'm not sure we realize just how much input we have in the joy of others merely by creating an environment that makes them feel loved and able to be who they are. Today we talk about being our 'unapologetic selves', but what if we never felt the need to apologize in the first place?

That to me is joy. I learned from them that there is no one way for Black boys and men to be, regardless of the messages I got from TV, music, books and the people around me. The pressure I placed on myself to live up to expectations wasn't something I had to deal with any more. Do you know how freeing that is? Do you know how much space that creates for the things that make you happy? The scope that gives you to actually learn about who you are at your core? The ways in which you are able to meet others emotionally? I was given room to be soft so I could have the energy to be strong when I needed to be. The specific type of freedom they provided me began my road to self-acceptance, and it's one of the reasons why I am here today.

Obviously, friendship groups are not a cure for everything. And, as life does for many teens, things change and the shape of friendships shift. As we grew up, we remained close, but we started seeing each other less due to work, personal circumstances and exploring other parts of ourselves. I moved into early adulthood armed with the lessons I gained from them and soon met the whirlwind that is my best friend, Bianca, who has been the source of so much happiness for me for well over a decade.

Bianca taught me a lot about masculinity as a grown man. I can imagine that being a foreign concept for some, given she is a woman. But you see, she is the person who has reconnected me to my core every time I've attempted to disconnect from it and put the mask back on to cope. During my first heartbreak, losing loved ones, issues with other friends, poor self-esteem – through all the things that can plunge you into a spiral of toxicity – our friendship has been a constant reminder of the importance of embracing my truest self. Loving myself and providing space for myself in the way we do with each other. Once you are taught the standard of *real* friendship, you don't settle for anything that falls short.

Our connection couldn't be described as anything other than fate. We first met in passing through a mutual friend and happened to be in the same nightclub weeks later. I remember walking up to her and saying, 'You're Bianca, right?', to which she covered her name tattoo and, in the most no-nonsense East End accent, replied, 'Yeh? How do you know and who are you?' (which is pretty on-brand). Following that initial shock, we ended up speaking about our lives for the rest of the night. We have been inseparable ever since. I have truly found a soulmate.

Bianca and I became notorious as a duo and formed an impenetrable bubble of joy that no one could burst. In each other we gained someone we could say the most outrageous things to without judgement, because, let's face it, a form of joy is being able to laugh at the things you'd probably get cancelled for with someone you trust. We each have someone who will be there no matter what happens, and who will swear and shout through the whole experience with us. Someone who would protect the other's value in any given situation at any given time. Someone who would safeguard the other's well-being without a second thought. Bianca also reminded me that I didn't have to be nice if a situation didn't deserve or require it. She was an antidote to the things that forced me to shrink myself and the bravado that acted as my safety mechanism. There is this expectation placed on many Black people to present themselves in a way that is palatable – not too loud, not too crude, not too direct – while maintaining strength. It's something reinforced by people outside and inside our communities. I gained the confidence to laugh in the face of people who tried to break me. I had started embracing who I was in my late teens, but my friendship with

Bianca in my early twenties taught me how to truly show up for myself.

It's important to recognize that when people talk about Black Boy Joy or Black Girl Joy, it isn't infantilization. For many, myself included, it is regaining elements of our childhoods that we lost or had ripped away from us for one reason or another. It is reminding ourselves to honour our inner child; that we are deserving of the childlike joy that comes with innocence; that joy isn't reserved for people who don't look like us. For many Black men especially, it's being able to celebrate a version of masculinity that gives us freedom and also serves us and those around us wholly. One that is unique to each of us in all of its brilliance and complexity. My friendship with Bianca is a testament to this. We have both experienced things that meant we had to grow up quickly, and our playfulness means we can honour those children that live inside us.

I wish I could share all our stories with you but, really, they will probably have to go in a memoir one day when I no longer have to be an 'upstanding' somebody. For insight, though, one of my fondest memories is a mutual friend coming to pick us up after we were spotted lying in a park laughing at 1 p.m., having not been home from a nightclub. We are ridiculous, but we look out for each other fiercely and understand each other deeply. We laugh our way through some of our most difficult experiences and have quickly become joy embodied for each other, and we understand that laughing through difficult experiences isn't a harmful coping mechanism but a way to process. We can talk to each other about our deepest feelings, cry them out and laugh about them later. We speak after therapy sessions to debrief.

Alongside therapy, I did a lot of reflecting before I wrote down my thoughts and feelings for you. My relationship with joy is a complicated one, and I wanted to give you something real in the hope that you are able to locate joy within yourself. I think we get caught in the performance of joy rather than the feeling. We have the perfect words, the perfect aesthetics, the award-winning performances to show the world we are as carefree as humanly possible. But is it something we completely embody? Do we ask ourselves what joy looks like outside of what we are told it should? Beyond the restrictions and labels thrown at us? When the books are finished, when the apps are closed, when the music stops, when the noise ceases and we are lying there alone in stillness, engulfed in our silence, are we seeking out not only the joy we deserve but the joy that serves us?

I want to remind you that, whoever you are, you are deserving of joy and you should go where you are loved, held and accepted whenever and wherever possible. Joy should never be something you need to give up pieces of yourself for – you should be able to grasp it with every part of who you are while those that love you hold you up. I've learned how to remove my mask. I hope you will too.

FIND YOUR OWN JOY

Pick up your phone, open a new message, select the name of someone who found or healed a piece of you and tell them you love them.

The Power Within

Finding purpose
in raising my voice

Leigh-Anne Pinnock

SINGER-SONGWRITER,
ACTRESS & ENTREPRENEUR

My name is Leigh-Anne Pinnock. I would say I'm best known for being a member of the biggest girl band in the world, Little Mix. You might think you already know a lot about me, but there's something new I want to share with you. Over the past three years, I have been on a life-changing journey that's been an alchemy of self-love and self-belief. It has led me to find my power, my purpose and my Black joy.

In 1979, my parents, John and Debbie, met at a party in Edmonton, London. They got together and later decided to buy a house in High Wycombe. They married in 1990 and a year later I was born – the last of three girls. I can honestly say I was blessed in regard to my upbringing. If I wanted something, my parents would work extremely hard to make it happen. We travelled abroad at least once a year and we were enrolled in everything from horse riding to stage school. My dad even turned our garage into a dance studio.

Where I would say my upbringing differed from many other mixed-race children is that both of my parents are mixed race too. Both my grandfathers were part of the Windrush generation. My paternal grandfather, Steve, journeyed over from Jamaica, and my mum's dad, Martin Luther, came from Barbados. They settled in England and married white British women, Norma and Doreen, my late grandmothers. It's hard to put into words how being a second-generation mixed-race woman has impacted the way I identify, but for you I'll give it a go. Having two mixed-race parents and being raised within a household where Caribbean culture sat at the core, I never struggled to understand my identity. I know I am essentially mixed race but, in essence, I've always identified as being Black.

For as long as I can remember, we've travelled to Jamaica as a family at least once a year to visit our relatives. Jamaica is like my second home and there is nowhere else on earth that gives me that sense of belonging. No matter how busy my schedule is, I still make time to ensure I can keep up the trips, and every time I leave a bit of my heart and soul there. Besides our visits to Jamaica, our household was shaped by my mother's childhood traditions. Every Saturday we would have Saturday Soup, a delicious beef soup with thyme and dumplings, and on Sunday we would have a roast with rice and peas. Traditionally my dad would always want my mum to cook the rice and peas with kidney beans, whereas my mum's Barbadian roots meant she would prefer gungo peas. Both were equally tasty.

But while I was clear on my personal identity, the way I was brought up didn't quite equip me with the strength to deal with the experiences I would later face. Experiences that, for a while, meant I struggled to find happiness.

I can't remember ever wanting to be anything else but a popstar. My sisters and I were told by our family that we could be and achieve anything. Our motto, preached especially by my Grandad Steve, has always been, 'We're Pinnocks.' There was a pride and strength that came with being in the Pinnock family. But, despite this, as a child I was the shyest little thing you'd ever seen. I'd cling on tightly to my dad whenever anyone I didn't know tried to interact with me, and I used to always say, 'I hate peoples.' It's probably not a surprise to learn that I was never the confident stage-school kid, despite being enrolled in one from the age of seven.

Nevertheless, something drew me to the spotlight, leading me to enter every talent show in school. I was always so nervous and would sing to the floor, avoiding eye contact with the judges and the audience and playing my backing track way too loud – so you couldn't even hear my soft little high-pitched voice. But I still loved every second of it, and as I got older it was apparent that I actually had a good voice. The more people complimented me, the more my confidence and desire to become a popstar flourished. I believed it would happen and I remember being so inspired by shows like *Cleopatra* and *Sister, Sister*. Seeing young Black girls shine made me feel like my dream was accessible. The dream lived within me right through to secondary school. It never felt out of reach; there was no other option. I was manifesting without even knowing it.

The whole *X Factor* experience was surreal. We all auditioned as solo artists originally, but during the boot-camp stage the judges decided to form us into a girl band. I had never imagined myself in a group, but from the moment we sang together it was so clear that it was meant to be. More importantly, we clicked in every way and formed a strong friendship from the outset. Every week we overcame the girl-band curse, went on to reach the final and then became the first group to ever win the show. I couldn't stop pinching myself. I felt like I was living in a fantasy and at any moment I would wake up and realize it was all a dream. But it was very real – I'd done it!

Just like that, my life changed. After winning, everything happened so fast. I started to live what was my dream: the life of a popstar. Overnight I went from being a part-time waitress living with my mum to being part of a highly anticipated girl band that was set to be as big as the Spice Girls. I moved out of High Wycombe within months and rented a swanky penthouse apartment in London. We went on to travel the world and break records, and I bought my first house, met the man of my dreams and later was able to pay off my dad's mortgage and buy my mum a house too.

To the outside world I was living the dream, but inside I quickly began to feel lost. As the months and years went by, I felt like every other girl in the band mastered their identity and that they were all loved and embraced for it. They built their own fan bases and this was often highlighted at concerts and events where fans would stand and queue to take a picture with their favourite. I didn't feel that love. I felt like the toy that no one wanted to play with, the orange creme left in the Quality Street tin at Christmas, not quite to the taste of the majority. It was hard to speak up about this feeling because I still didn't quite know how to articulate *why* I felt like this. I would try and speak to my family and friends, but their response was often along the lines of: 'You're all paid the same, get on with it.'

I kept telling myself, 'It's OK, Leigh-Anne. It's probably going to take some time to build up your personal fan base, just keep smiling, keep working and putting on a brave face.' No one in the band or within management really understood the magnitude of how this weighed me down. I became more conscious of things that justified why I felt so out of place. At live events I would pick up on the fact that my name was not screamed as much as the other girls', and I would get anxious about meet-and-greets because I would often be ignored. As time went on, the feeling of not belonging grew to the point that I started to doubt my capabilities and thought that the world viewed me as the least talented band member.

We have been together touching ten years, so I would like to think by now people are able to identify me by my name as opposed to 'the Black one', 'the mixed one' or, worst of all, 'What's that one called again? Jade?' When this happened the first few times, I wasn't affected by it because it could have been a genuine mistake. But after a while it takes its toll. I've lost count of the number of occasions where I would walk on set with my bandmates, and the photographer or journalist would forget or mistake my name. I would often be the only Black person in these spaces too.

Years went by and I continued to struggle. I then reached the point where I knew I had been having this feeling for far too long; I needed to stop putting it to the back of my mind and start dismantling it. I thought back to something said to me by the American director and choreographer Frank Gatson: 'You're the Black girl, you have to work ten times harder.' In all honesty, at the time I was taken aback – I just didn't get it. But in recent years Frank's comment has begun to make sense: throughout my whole career I have felt that I needed to work that much harder in order to have the same acceptance and acknowledgement as my peers.

I started to read more, including *Why I'm No Longer Talking to White People About Race* by Reni Eddo-Lodge, which will stay with me forever. During this journey of discovery, I came across a quote that really resonated with me, though I'm at a loss to remember who said or wrote this: 'When a Black woman walks into a room of white people you would expect her to stand out, when really she is overlooked and disregarded.' It helped me understand why I had felt all these emotions about our Little Mix fan base. And in understanding them, I learned how to overcome them. I accepted that the reality was this: I was a Black girl in a girl band trying to make her mark within a white-dominated industry. I was therefore treated and looked at differently. I was experiencing racism. At this point, I started to build friendships with more Black creatives. It was healing to hear about their personal experiences within white-dominated industries. I found great comfort in learning that I wasn't alone.

My Nanny Doreen raised five mixed-race children in the 1960s and her mantra was: 'Teach your children love and the world will teach them to hate.' It meant that my dad wasn't given 'the talk'. He was never told that the colour of his skin might mean that he'd be subjected to racism. He lived by this and raised me and my sisters the same way. While we were educated on Black history and grew up thinking we were very in touch with our culture, we were unaware of the depths of racism or that we could be subjected to it. Growing up and nurturing my dream, I never for one second thought that my experience would be different to that of white popstars. Mel B was my favourite of the Spice Girls, but I didn't wonder if she experienced racism until I walked in her shoes. I won *The X Factor* and started my Little Mix journey never for one minute thinking that because I was a Black woman standing next to white women I would be the least valued, the least loved and the least desired.

So what could I do about it? Keep quiet and use what I had overcome only for the benefit of myself? Or speak out with the knowledge I had acquired? I chose the latter. In 2018, an opportunity came along to be interviewed, during which I was able to touch on my personal experiences within the group. For the first time, I tried to speak out publicly about how being seen as 'the Black girl' in the group had impacted me. At this moment, it felt like the entertainment world wasn't ready to talk about race, so what I said didn't grab the media's attention. I was relieved to have articulated my experiences for the first time publicly, but I still felt like I was carrying pain. I wasn't done.

Having now learned that what Frank Gatson said was in fact true, I knew I could either embrace and showcase my Black identity or carry an underlying sadness around and allow it to continue to fester. At this point in my life, I understood that being the Black girl within a pop band meant that I would always cater to the minority, not the majority. I understood that I wouldn't be everyone's first choice or favourite, and I was able to finally embrace my position within the group, not doubt it.

Then came the most joyous moment of my Little Mix career: a trip to Brazil. None of us were prepared for the reception we were about to receive. The airport was heaving with fans of all ethnicities, something I had never seen before while on tour. Our arrival went viral and we were flooded with messages from fans pouring out their hearts and thanking me for being such an inspiration. When we got to the hotel, we found fans queuing outside. I had to go and meet them.

Stepping out into the street to screams, I found around four hundred people all lined up behind barriers. They were waving handmade posters and holding gift bags. I remember one gift was a Brazil football shirt with my name on the back. I started at the top of the line and worked my way down to the bottom; I wanted to ensure I didn't miss a single person. The fans thanked me for staying true to myself and choosing to use my platform to educate my followers about police brutality; racism runs deep in Brazil and heavily impacts the Black and brown communities. Speaking up about my experiences and choosing to use my platform to raise awareness resonated with them.

There was a particular fan I spoke to whom I will never forget. He thanked me for being an advocate for the Black community and told me that I gave him strength and hope. I remember feeling so overwhelmed that I just couldn't hold the tears back. I wiped my tears away and the lady next to him called me a queen. I felt embraced for being myself, for being the Black girl, for the first time.

The following day we had our performance at the GRLS! Festival. It changed my life. I took a moment on stage to express my appreciation for the welcome we had received and the crowd started cheering 'LEIGH-ANNE! LEIGH-ANNE! LEIGH-ANNE!' Never in my whole career had I been given

" I have found my voice and **I choose to use it "**

such a reception from a country next to my bandmates. Brazil welcomed me, they loved me, and thanks to them I came home more confident than ever.

Two months later, on 25 May 2020, the world learned about the death of George Floyd and the Black Lives Matter movement accelerated. Everyone was talking about race. I have always seen my personal experience within the music industry as a reflection of how the world can view Black people, but I also understood that what I faced was tiny compared to the racism that exists elsewhere. I knew it was important not to make the conversation about just me because the reality is that being light-skinned brings its own privilege, and I'm conscious that dark-skinned women in the industry face even more barriers to success. But, even so, I knew I had to speak out. I hoped I could relate to people and restart the conversation I had tried to ignite before.

I decided to upload a video to my Instagram touching on my experiences but more importantly talking about systemic racism. The support was mind-blowing and I took great comfort in knowing I wasn't alone. Other celebrities decided to follow suit and I had so many people reach out to thank me for giving them the inspiration. Not only had I overcome my own insecurities but I had also found a way to empower other people who had been subjected to racism.

Nothing can prepare you for the feeling you may have as

the only Black person at the table or at the party, but what I have learned is that loving yourself wholeheartedly before you wish to be loved by others gives you power. Overall, my journey to becoming the woman I am now was emotional and painful – unbearable at times – but the one thing I managed to find and hold on to was my power. I am no longer the girl who gets anxious before fan events. I am no longer the girl who questions my position and purpose. I have found my voice and I choose to use it. When I look back at recordings of me performing in the early days, I no longer recognize the girl desperate to be appreciated.

It's OK to not be to everyone's taste – just ensure you are your own favourite flavour. What I needed to believe ten years ago was, yes, you're the Black girl, so embrace it, own it and be an unapologetic representation of your culture. I found my power when I realized it was within me, within my skin and within my soul the whole time. It just needed to be set free.

FIND YOUR OWN JOY

Introduce Manifest Mondays to your weekly routine. Whether it's attending the gym three times or finishing that assignment, take time every Monday to think about what you want to accomplish that week.

" I found my power
when I realized it
was within me,
within my skin
and within my soul,
the whole time.
**It just needed
to be set free** "

Fresh Trim
The babble and buzz of the barbershop

Tope Olufemi
JOURNALIST, MUSICIAN & STUDENT

Illustration by Olivia Twist

I've been going to the same north London barbershop since I've had hair on my head. Each visit begins with the same question: 'How's Dad?'

The barbers remember him bringing me in after football matches to get my hair cut when I was younger. Sometimes he'd have something done too – before he lost his hair at least. Mostly, he'd sit and wait with me, quietly proud of how little trouble I was in the chair. He didn't speak much, keeping his phrases short and deliberate, yet I found myself learning from both his words and his actions: how he'd carry himself in the shop, the way he spoke to others. He taught me about communicating with people through his friendliness, his eagerness to begin a conversation, to introduce himself to others. It was a rare moment for us to be together, where we sometimes discussed tactics for the next football game or how school was going.

There's a loudness that's unique to the barbershop: the hum of the TV in the background, barbers shouting across the room to each other. Hairspray and cologne filling the air, mixing in with the conversation to create an atmosphere that feels homely. The wall-to-wall mirrors reflecting familiar Black faces. I vaguely remember the conversations my dad would have with the barbers, about business back in Nigeria, the stresses of work, the ease of religion. I also remember being way too young to understand any of those things, though I found comfort in their conversation, and craning my neck slightly to see what was playing on the TV while hoping that this trip would be rewarded with a visit to McDonald's. Since I grew old enough to go alone, they've never failed to ask how he's doing.

I didn't really fear getting my hair cut when I was younger. I was always tall for my age, so my legs would fit comfortably on the seat, and the mohawk I donned around the age of ten made trips to the barbershop every month or so a lot of fun. It was a place where I could express myself. I associated it with 'looking good', or whatever that means when you're a child. I'd ask the barber for little lines on the side too, trying to fit in. I remember going to school and matches feeling uniquely proud of my appearance, how distinctly 'me' it felt. Sometimes, when waiting to get my hair cut, my eyes would frantically dart across the outdated posters of Black men with fresh haircuts (possibly from the early 1990s), each one numbered, as if I wasn't going to choose the exact same style I'd had for years.

The first time you exert any real control over your life as a child is through experimenting with your hair. Getting my hair cut in my signature mohawk was symbolic for me; it made me who I was and matched my loud, bubbly personality. The tall, chubby kid with the glasses and the mohawk became my brand throughout my childhood, and,

Olivia Twist

looking back, it represented me well.

Adolescence brought a new phase of experimentation. I started letting my hair grow – then decided to cut it all off again. The breeze I felt across my head on the way to school after a fresh trim was a brief new beginning, and my barbers followed me on the journey to figuring out just what style would work for me. When you're much younger, personal grooming isn't all that important; after all, you're surrounded by children just learning how to wipe their noses and clean their mouths. Moving into secondary school made me aware of the value of taking care of your appearance. I learned that clean-shaven heads were a no-go after falling victim to jokes about my bald head – and a few friendly slaps.

Black British boys cycle through different hairstyles during school: coming in after the weekend and seeing your friend has had his hair cut; wondering which level it was so you can ask your barber for the same. Growing your hair out for a high-top; cutting it low for some waves. Imitating US rappers' pioneering twists; stashing afro combs and gel in bags, soon to be confiscated by teachers who didn't get just how much Black hair means to Black people. Hair and Black identity are tied together so tightly that there's a hyper-awareness of how it looks. Much of your status in school hinges on how good your hair looks. Your barber holds your social life in his hands with every cut and you trust them with that, every time.

In the chair, you often find that your mind is full of thoughts. You would expect the forty-five minutes you spend waiting for the sting of the alcohol on your neck at the end of your haircut to be relatively idle, but instead you might be thinking: *Why is this man shouting on the phone to his friend in the middle of my shape-up?*, *Is this what my hair is supposed to look like right now?*, *I can't see the TV – who's winning?* or *I might have to wear a hat after this one.*

I learned the value of trusting your barber when I let my uncle cut my hair in an attempt to fit in with my peers. I needed a line-up, so when he enthusiastically told me he could cut hair I saw an easy solution. He so often fixed our broken appliances and helped me sew busted trousers that I imagined his far-reaching talents would extend to shape-ups. When I got to school the following week and heard the name 'Joan of Arc' due to how curved my hairline was, I knew I had a problem on my hands. Needless to say, once the barbers at the shop saw my hair a few days later, they declared it an emergency. I was immediately sat down ahead of others in the line, and they worked their magic, managing to restore my hairline to its former glory. I didn't have a grasp of what a bad haircut really was until I looked at myself after the life-saving surgery and saw the difference – and vowed to never let a relative near me with clippers again. After this, I knew that if I ever needed a cut, the barbers were the go-to, no matter the circumstance. They'd seen me at my lowest and withheld judgement; I knew they cared.

The communal aspects of the barbershop are what foster its intimacy: the uncle in the corner who is always there but whom you never see getting his hair cut; the quiet roar of a football match on the weekends; arguments about said football match being had loudly across the shop; the aunties in the hairdresser's within the barbershop having conversations among themselves. The same hand resting at the back of your neck that has rested there for years, the same technique, the comfortable closeness. It feels like home.

'What about your sister?' is the new question at my barbershop. My older sister gets her hair done by the same barber as me, so he often asks when she'll be back for another trim. I never know when, but the question cheers me enough that I'll always relay it to her when I get home. The smaller details they always seem to remember about the way you like your haircuts, even caring to remember to ask about family, make experiences at the barbershop all the more special. Once you have a favourite barber, you spend time competing for his attention, whether it's calling to let him know you're planning to come that day or waiting three hours for the fourteen other people he has to finish first. You sit in his chair and he treats you like you're the only person he's ever cut in his life.

This familiarity also manifests in other ways. The Black

barbershop is a place for those who've emigrated from their homes in Africa or the Caribbean to feel a sense of peace that often isn't afforded to them in this country. Immigrants can speak their native languages as loudly as they want without judgement. They can hear their music play, tell stories and eat food from their home country. My barbershop had an African–Caribbean restaurant two doors down and the barbers would often get their lunch from there. Ultimately, the barbershop shelters those within it from the racism that runs rampant outside. In the barbershop, you're not falling victim to a toxic work environment that vilifies and demeans the very things that create Black joy, nor suffering at the hands of a government that deports people into precarity – and sometimes to their death.

The barbershop remains a site of Black British history and culture, acting as a safe space for those who frequently visit. Inua Ellams's fantastic play *Barber Shop Chronicles* represents these ideas in real time, travelling to Johannesburg, Harare, Kampala, Lagos, Accra and London to show the diversity of the barbershop experience, while demonstrating how Blackness ties them all together. Before seeing this play, I'd rarely considered the barbershop in this way. It was only when I began to understand the culture that surrounded me as a British–Nigerian that it became obvious just how important the barbershop is for Black people across generations. It's a site of cultural production, with endless oral histories weaving their way across its space.

Ellams's play made clear to me how the barbershop offers a unique space for Black masculine-presenting people to find refuge, care and joy. It's a space to gist, free from the weight of judgement that wider society places on their backs. It's a space where people get to share and attempt to understand each other. It's a space where they can have intimate conversations about how Blackness shapes their everyday lives or lighter conversations about the films they watched that week and the parts of their native country they miss. In a world where they feel silenced, the barbershop encourages its residents to speak.

In fact, participating in conversations that may not be had elsewhere, expressing both frustration and joy, is one of the fundamental underpinnings of the Black barbershop. It would be nothing without the words that flow through it or the stories that are told. Black people in this country have suffered relentlessly and have often had spaces of refuge and solace stripped away from them. Homes have been lost, entire histories erased, but the barbershop remains one fixed aspect of the Black British experience. For a community with poor collective mental health, the barbershop provides a home away from home, a space free from racialized preconceptions. Our pain and trauma are not trivialized here, as they so often are elsewhere.

"In a world where Black people feel silenced, **the barbershop encourages its residents to speak**"

For me, this intimacy has remained free of boundaries. In my late teens, I began to deviate from the masculine norms that once defined me. I stopped playing football and started dyeing my hair, wearing earrings and generally realizing that I felt a disconnect between traditional masculinity and my presentation. I often worried about the repercussions this would bring for me within the barbershop, but they never manifested. I was greeted with the same queries about my father, the same rough hand guiding my head away from the TV screen, the same bright white lights and smell of hairspray.

A haircut for me is transformative in the most subtle way, and I know this feeling resonates with many. You start taking more pictures of yourself and your confidence is boosted. The forty-five minutes you spend in the shop can change you entirely. But ultimately it's a joy that transcends the body. It does not live or die by the way that we look but is merely represented through our skin fades or locs. The barbershop is a safe haven; it represents something that's simultaneously immovable, defiant and joyful. It has helped me understand the cultural significance of space within the Black community, mainly because we as a community lack these spaces. It's allowed me to reimagine what Black joy looks and feels like, how it is present in the everyday, the fact that it can be subtle. It doesn't have to be excellent; it can be casual and mundane.

The barbershop has taught me that if you listen beyond the babble and buzz, you might experience Black joy in a new, exciting way.

FIND YOUR OWN JOY

Reminisce with friends about your worst haircuts, your favourite barbers or hairdressers and the best you've felt post-trim.

Young Black Kings

Celebrating my heroes

Athian Akec

ACTIVIST & WRITER

We are blessed to be living in what could be the Black British Renaissance. My greatest source of joy is the work of Black artists. On the most difficult and stressful of days, I'll turn to their art to remind myself that we can build a different and better world. As a young Black person born in the early 2000s, I am exposed to the work of Black British figures who are pushing boundaries and reaching higher than ever before. A new generation is rising and they are uncompromising in their Blackness. This essay is written for them: the people who are striving for our stories to be told, our perspectives to be heard, who are pushing for the progress we desperately need. It's also for the communities who teach them, hold them up and give us all strength. It's for our Black heroes.

It's almost a weekly ritual that I watch the video to the Caleb Femi poem 'Secret Life of Gs'. It shows young Black men surrounded by nature – something we rarely ever see in art. It opens with the words: 'You all know what it is to live in such a place where everything works against you – the policies, the politics, the police, the news, the teachers, the bloody weather. Tell me you haven't thought about escaping it.' As young Black men from working-class backgrounds, the way my friends and I are presented in the media is overwhelmingly negative. Here, Caleb articulates the need for a future that allows young Black men to live fulfilled, safe and joyful lives. He says:

Take me away from the block
Where the sunrise has a different accent
And we crack smiles not bones
Where there are more trees than lampposts
More life in our shadows than ghosts

As I grow up it's becoming clearer that there's something empowering about your experiences and your way of looking at the world being validated. We need to know that the highs and lows of our lives aren't unique, incomprehensible or strange; that we are bonded with other people who can understand our lives without necessarily knowing us. I don't think any two people navigate the world or view it in an identical manner, but this validation is multi-layered. It's the way stories are told about people like you in art, but it's also having people who fight for your interests in political and activist spaces, and journalists who speak from your perspective.

Our perception of the past paints the way we view the present, and the power in how we collectively understand history should never be underestimated or minimized. More is being done to show the profound impact Black people have had on British society. There is an increasing focus on educating young people about the way colonialism, empire and slavery have shaped systemic racism; a clear example of this was the toppling of slave trader Edward Colston's statue in Bristol in

June 2020 and the public debate that followed. Black British historians like David Olusoga and Olivette Otele are waking us up to the often-forgotten reality that Black life in Britain stretches back centuries, that there were Black Victorians and Romans who lived full and complex lives.

My generation has the immense privilege of seeing the rise of Black public figures who reflect the diversity of our interests and humanity. We have Black writers and journalists who are bringing our stories to life like never before; we have Black actors who are taking centre stage; we have Black poets pushing forward the art form. We think of ourselves as being products of our own talents and efforts, but this couldn't be further from the truth. Behind everyone who has inspired me is a network of people who believed in them, invested time in them and gave them an opportunity.

Daniel Kaluuya's Oscar for his role as Black Panther activist Fred Hampton in *Judas and the Black Messiah* wouldn't have been possible without the free acting classes he got from the Anna Scher Theatre in north-west London. Akala's brilliant Oxford Union lecture on a thousand years of African history and bestselling book *Natives* wouldn't have been possible without the Pan-African Saturday school he attended as a child, which exposed him to the history of precolonial African societies and Black resistance. And Stormzy's immense cultural impact in multiple spheres, from

#Merky Books to the Stormzy Scholarship, wouldn't have been possible without a dedicated, talented team to bring his vision to life. Individualism would have us think these undoubtedly talented people had achieved what they have on their own, but this couldn't be further from the truth.

But as much as I think representation is important, it doesn't replace the need to fight to improve conditions for all Black people. Our right to live a life of dignity, safety and fulfilment should not be dependent on beating enormous statistical odds but a guarantee we all have as humans. As much as we should value and uplift individuals, to find our joy as a generation we have to move into a space where Black mediocrity is valued as much as Black excellence. The fixation we see on excellence, as well-intentioned as it may be, is leading to a reality where people's perspectives are being influenced by respectability politics.

I see this in the enormous pressure we feel as young Black people to be successful in academic or sporting settings in order to even compete in a society where systemic racism constantly threatens our sanity and safety. I try to navigate the world with a balance of optimism and realism. I know that British politics would be far less dysfunctional if it were truly representative of the country and not as heavily dominated by Oxbridge grads. But as a young Black man trying to exist in these spaces, I don't have the privilege of being disengaged.

"As much as we should value and uplift individuals, to find our joy as a generation we have to move into a space where **Black mediocrity is valued as much as Black excellence**"

At the time of writing this essay, I'm trying to not mess up my A levels and will hopefully be taking up a place at Cambridge to study history. The application process was one of the most difficult things I've ever done. The three weeks before the final deadline, I was running on about four and a half hours sleep. The lockdown and the emotionally draining months of the Black Lives Matter protests made it difficult to prep for the application and interview. The reason why I pushed so hard is the same reason why some of my friends spend hours recording music or working to become elite athletes. There's a kind of quiet acknowledgement among young Black people that society will only afford you humanity if you exhibit extraordinary ability.

I have a right to be able to live a life where I'm not constantly threatened by the state and other people. Racism is irrational and is fundamentally rooted in the erasure of humanity. As Kano highlights in his album *Hoodies All Summer*, despite enormous success and recognition, there are constant issues Black people who reach the top face because of racism, and no level of achievement will change this. My hope is that we can one day ditch our obsession with Black excellence as it's clear that you can play by all the rules of respectability and still feel the hand of systemic racism. It reinforces the idea that those who face racism at the bottom of society are somehow 'deserving' and could have escaped its path through greater effort or ability.

Our heroes have their place in this fight too, despite what may seem like a contradiction. Even with the immense and disproportionate scrutiny, Black artists often play the role of political messengers. One of the most interesting parts of Black existence in public life is how many of our figures have utilized their platforms, sometimes explicitly, sometimes in a more low-key manner, to fight for the kind of progressive politics embodied by young people in this country. The arts have always been a space where voices drowned out from the political sphere can reflect the perspectives of marginalized people. These voices are stepping up to say what many are feeling but no one is echoing loud enough.

The American author and civil-rights activist Toni Cade Bambara said that 'the role of the artist is to make the revolution irresistible', and many Black British artists are presenting an alternative vision of the country that is more collectivist, where we are governed in the interests of everyone and not a select few. For me, two performances in particular speak the most to this reality: Dave's 2020 Brit Awards performance, where he called out Boris Johnson as 'a real racist'; and Stormzy's 2019 Glastonbury set, where he emerged in his now iconic Banksy-designed stab-proof vest and delivered a powerful performance that addressed racial injustice. And while the path to liberation and justice in this

" At its best, art reminds us to hold on to moments of joy and remember that **periods of struggle will pass** " country will not open up purely through the contributions of artists, they play a key role in reminding us that another future is possible, that there is space for what we think and feel, even if those in politics ignore it.

The importance of Black British art should never be minimized. In life we can often feel like our experiences and struggles as Black people are our own. Our stories for too long have been erased and sidelined, our creativity narrowed, our full range of humanity not given space. The greatest art articulates what we feel but don't have the words to say, the things we can recognize but that are just beyond the reach of our expression. At its best, art reminds us to hold on to moments of joy and remember that periods of struggle will pass.

The role that culture has played in Black activism is too often erased. The radical origins of Notting Hill Carnival have been forgotten. Politicians often dismiss the contributions of Black artists to political conversations, as seen with MP Michael Gove's condescending tweet ('I set trends dem man copy') in response to Stormzy's interventions during the 2019 general election. However, even though art can be a platform for societal change, it must never detract from the immense work needed to tackle injustice.

I can say first-hand as an activist that burnout is a major problem, and we as a generation will have to cultivate spaces where we can rest, have fun and embrace happiness. But that doesn't have to be divorced completely from the fight. As young people, the increasing presence of Black voices in journalism, activism and politics should push us to imagine a radically better future. Our imagination should reach for the broadest, biggest and boldest change possible. The scale of the crises we are living through – with the looming threat of climate change, the endless cycles of racial injustice and economic uncertainty – calls for us to embrace joy as a means of keeping up the fight for the solutions our communities desperately need.

We need new stories. We need systems that can bring justice, fairness and equality to the way society is run. We need to place community and care at the heart of what we do. The fight for these things will be hard, but it will always be worth it. But let's not forget that joy will play a huge part in our being able to build this new future. We have to envision a future beyond survival and cultivate a politics of hope. We need to remind ourselves that Black joy is exactly what we are fighting for.

FIND YOUR OWN JOY

Seek out Black art – in all its forms, including music and books – that gives you joy and offers escapism from your familiar world.

" We have to envision a future beyond survival and cultivate a politics of hope. We need to remind ourselves that **Black joy is exactly what we are fighting for** "

Blue Magic

Magic

The self-expressiveness

of Black beauty

Mikai McDermott

MULTI-DISCIPLINARY CREATIVE

'How many plaits do we have left?' I ask, aged ten, as I sit between my mother's knees on her bedroom floor. The cushion placed underneath my bum has long since flattened and I am ready to get up.

Memories like this have shaped much of my understanding of Black beauty. This was my first encounter with beauty as a child, where I learned that Black hair is a community effort. Our love for hair, and the practice of doing hair, brings us all together. Both my mother and my aunt, a hairdresser, were central to my initial interpretation of beauty; to feel beautiful was synonymous with feeling loved by them. I know that many young Black women share a similar experience to mine. We all vividly remember how it felt when our aunties and grandmothers smoothed our hair whenever we came to visit. In so many ways, my family taught me to take pride in my appearance. Now, in my twenties, I often think back to being seated between my mother's knees, Blue Magic grease on my scalp, while she knocked my head with the rat-tail comb for moving around too much, and how these small interactions between the women in my family spoke to larger themes of beauty in Black Caribbean communities.

The concept of beauty is a loaded one, created within hierarchies that oppress women in particular. Beauty, and attractiveness by extension, are ideas that I've been reckoning with and trying to dismantle. When we look at how Blackness connects with beauty, it becomes even more complex. Historically, European beauty standards have not included Blackness; they dismiss afro hair and dark skin as 'ugly'. It is through Black women's growing consciousness that we have been able to create our own beauty standards. Through an exploration of digital subcultures and engagement with other Black women worldwide, these new beauty standards have become personal. By rejecting European beauty standards, we have found our confidence as a community.

But in a world where we share so much of ourselves online, image takes centre stage. The dominance of social media has given rise to a new occupation: the influencer. These people are essentially walking advertisements, the new way for brands to market their beauty products to a more trusting audience. The influencer world has made the power of appearances more insidious. Discussions surrounding beauty are now heavily dependent on individualistic ideas of self-worth, where body and beauty have become a superficial form of liberation for young Black women who are hypervisible online. Even talking about prettiness as a means of empowerment obscures the structural realities of life for Black people and ignores the fact that there are material consequences for 'ugliness'. The way you are treated by other women in online spaces and whether you are regarded as desirable by straight cis men affects your self-esteem. Even more so, the connection of 'ugliness' to

Black beauty has made it so that Black people are not deemed worthy of space to tell our stories.

Black beauty binds and breaks us. It's a source of joy – and sometimes pain. It means so many things, some contradictory, but that is what makes it such a necessary concept to take, reckon with and rework every day. In her 2009 book *Black Beauty*, Professor Shirley Anne Tate highlights that Black beauty is 'your own acceptance of yourself as beautiful and a continuing uneasy interconnectedness with ideals of white beauty'. Over the past five years, especially when I was in my late teens, I've been working through the contradictions surrounding beauty expectations, giving them less power over my life. It's liberating knowing that beauty standards don't need to have such a hold over how I see myself and those around me.

When I was growing up, my aunt would canerow my natural hair every Sunday before the school week, right up until I was thirteen. It was an experience I loved. But suddenly it wasn't seen as cool to have natural hair. I would beg her and my mum for a relaxer, as I thought it would make my hair flow like the girls on the Dark and Lovely boxes. I know many of us can relate to this story and the massive hair breakage that occurs afterwards. I spent my late teens and early twenties growing my natural hair back from over-processing it. Through detaching my self-worth from my hair,

"It's liberating knowing that beauty standards **don't need to have such a hold over how I see myself and those around me**"

I was able to appreciate it for its beauty, regardless of what societal opinions were. Seeing my mother and aunt with short hairstyles definitely helped, as it taught me that length and thickness – two core facets of the mainstream natural hair movement – were not necessary to have beautiful hair. For them I am eternally grateful.

Natural hair knowledge has grown on social media in recent years and Black people have been creating spaces online to exist freely, celebrate themselves and practise radical self-care. The natural hair movement has reclaimed an aspect of the collective Black identity, showing how the afro is a politicized symbol of Blackness that resists white beauty standards. It signifies a cultural acceptance within Black communities that did not exist to the same extent before, and it is incredibly exciting to see.

But natural hair isn't the only form of self-expression for Black people. Wigs, weaves and hair extensions have also helped us experiment with our looks. I wear my hair in all of these styles; not only are they a form of self-expression but they each communicate a different part of my identity as a Black Caribbean woman in Britain. I love protective styling because natural hair thrives with hairstyles that keep hydration in. Braids and canerows were a simple protective hairstyle worn by enslaved women on plantations. They reconciled the idea of Black hair as a community effort.

As well as the communal aspect, small grains could be kept within these hairstyles for sustenance and even for survival. Newer styles like wigs and weaves have provided ease – and assimilation in some cases – and given a substantial boost to the Black beauty economy. While some might consider wearing weaves and wigs to be giving in to white beauty standards, I believe beauty has allowed some to navigate violently anti-Black structures. I know how rigid Western beauty ideals are, and, because of this, I'm not asking Black women to 'give in' to them. Instead, I want us to reconsider the ways beauty politics have placed anti-Black ideas about our bodies in our minds. More importantly, I ask for us to continue to reimagine the parameters of beauty for ourselves.

I love digging into Black British history because it reminds me that Black people intentionally finding empowerment through beauty isn't a new phenomenon. In the 1950s, there was an understanding within Caribbean communities arriving in Britain that there would not be salons that could do Black hair, so they relied on each other to fix their hair at home. The first Black woman to establish a communal space for Black hair in Britain was Trinidadian pianist Winifred Atwell, who set up a salon in Brixton specifically to train white English women to understand afro hair. At the same time, there was the rise of anti-imperialist independence movements in the late 1950s alongside the growing Black Power movement. Doing their hair at home became a solution many Black women found, and these trends are still seen today in contemporary discourses on Black hair. Like with my mother and aunty, at-home hairdressing created a safe space for me as a young Black girl and showed me how important it was to have a community of Black femmes around me. The communal nature of Black hair predates the transatlantic slave trade, but it is interesting to see how marginalized communities have created ways to assimilate into new societies.

Learning how Caribbean women before me created their own metaphorical geographies has been crucial to my understanding of beauty. In getting to know the ways that community-building and beauty go hand in hand, I have come to terms with my position – both as a Black Caribbean woman and previously as a hairstylist and creator. Seeing the communal aspect of Black hair was my entire childhood: growing up in my aunt's salon every weekend while my mother taught at Saturday school meant seeing countless Black women leave with an array of hairstyles. Eight-year-old me was fascinated, to say the least, and I would pass the time by braiding mannequin heads and pestering my aunt to do my hair. When I grew older and my aunt no longer needed to babysit me, I began to realize that hair had formed a huge part of my childhood, that I associated it with love and nurture and that it was what I wanted to do.

I've also been inspired by how women such as afro hairstylist Charlotte Mensah and beauty entrepreneur Sharmadean Reid have used hair and beauty as tools of financial empowerment, creating new forms of self-expression and self-acceptance. By curating spaces that allow Black women to find confidence through beauty, they are helping offset the insidious nature of online beauty standards. These women have influenced me to see my beauty in a more positive light. As the founder of WAH Nails and Beauty Stack, Sharmadean encourages women to empower themselves through beauty networks and stresses the importance of economic independence. Charlotte has given validity to Black women who specialize in textured hair, wigs and weaves, and she's the reason why I became a hairstylist. These women have shown me why it is necessary for us to personalize our experiences with the concept of beauty. Taking a one-size-fits-all approach does not address the nuances of the Black British experience.

Creating hair experiences for clients has allowed me to find my feet in the beauty sphere and understand how hair shapes the way people see themselves. I see how many wholesome relationships have developed from meeting new clients, how I have managed to create a safe space for Black femmes. There have been clients trying out a new protective style with me for the first time and I get to witness their excitement at seeing themselves in a new way. There are others who get the same style time and time again, but equally this is how they choose to present themselves, a way to affirm their identity. Seeing how hair has so many meanings for different women inspires me to continue reimagining Black beauty, both for myself, as a hypervisible Black woman, and for my community.

I understand how important hair is for Black women, how heavily politicized it is, and how markedly different our experiences are. I also know how empowered beauty and beauty networks make me feel. This is why I think it is important for us to be safely visible within British beauty communities. The cost of hypervisibility is high, but this can be counteracted by creating supportive networks in the Black British community.

We can also start doing the work of changing Black beauty standards by doing away with internalized shame. The explanations that maintain the status quo for beauty standards keep Black beauty as an afterthought. Undoing this means taking steps to recognize the intersections that dictate the lives of Black people and continuing beyond the limits of Western feminism, which is centred around wealthy white women.

In 'Dis Place', Caribbean poet Marlene Nourbese Philip writes, 'Dis place is not my home.' We can use this as a metaphor for mainstream beauty standards – they are not our safe space. Shirley Anne Tate says it best: let's 'leave behind essentialist ideas of Blackness which are only capable of coming into being through whiteness'. Let us be proactive in seeing ourselves outside of mainstream beauty standards. Consciously decentring whiteness in conversations about beauty means we can truly understand the fullness of the Black beauty experience. There is so much to be found when we look inward and to each other for affirmation and love. I think back to the intimacy of my hair and beauty experiences with my aunt and mother, how they shaped my understanding of race and gender.

Black British beauty conversations include so many complexities. At the centre of the discussion on Black beauty lies an important question: how do you feel and realize your own beauty? It's a question I find myself constantly interacting with in a multitude of ways. It forces me to grapple with the paradoxical nature of beauty. It also makes me feel hopeful that I can imagine a new future for Black British beauty.

FIND YOUR OWN JOY

Try out a new hairstyle that you've always wanted to do but have been afraid to make the leap. Transform yourself!

66 There is so much to be found when **we look inward and to each other for affirmation and love 99**

A Stomach Like Mine

Fatness as happiness

Sophia Tassew

CONTENT CREATOR & DESIGNER

Fat joy. Two words I would have never imagined could be linked together. It's taken time, though – years and years for me to get to a space where I truly experience pockets of joy in my body.

As well as being the backbone of body positivity – a social movement dedicated to fat acceptance and the equal treatment of fat bodies in all areas of life – Black fat women online are probably the main reason why I'm able to function in many things that I do. I actually remember the first time I saw a Black plus-size model on Instagram. I was around nineteen years old and lying in bed, submerged in my duvet; the lights were off and I was endlessly scrolling. I was stopped in my tracks by a black-and-white photo of a Black woman who had a stomach like mine wearing a black gown. She seemed so comfortable in front of the camera, as if it were no big deal. To me, she had done the most groundbreaking thing I had seen online: she was simply being herself. That was one of my earliest memories of seeing a fat Black body presented in such a beautiful way – unlike seeing someone in a fat suit in a comedy – and linking my own body with beauty. My view of the world changed from that night onwards. I'm not sure if what I experienced in that moment was joy, but somehow I think I knew that there would be joy in my future.

I was raised in Peckham, south-east London, and it shaped major parts of who I am today. I went to an all-girls school, which sat right at the end of Peckham Rye Park. It wasn't for the faint of heart, but I always felt that my experiences there were good for my development. The girls who bullied me day in and day out were brutal, but I honestly don't think I would have been as creative as I am now, or maintained a certain level of integrity, if I had grown up differently from the way I did. It gave me skin thick enough to withstand fat jokes from guys. And attending an all-girls school makes you an expert in relationships with other women.

Bullying in school came in different forms: sometimes it was overt and other times it was disguised as 'banter'. My weight was mentioned in every argument and the entire class would whoop and holler in support of whoever called me the F-word. Back then, fat was the last thing you wanted to be. I would be eating my lunch, minding my business, and someone would comment on how much I was enjoying my food, knowing full well that it would embarrass me.

I was the friend everyone turned to when they had body issues, and at age fifteen I felt like I was the Year 10 body-image therapist when I barely had support myself. Perhaps because everyone saw how much stick I got for being fat, they thought I could take on their issues too. I was experiencing all of this before I was introduced to the world of body positivity. I had no sense of who I was or pride in myself. I grew up thinking my body was wrong and that by a certain age I had to look a certain way or I had failed. Looking back at that now, I ask myself, 'Failed *what* exactly? Life?' I had spent my most innocent years already putting a timer on my joy. The media perpetuated diet culture, which fuelled negative attitudes towards fat bodies. It took a long time for me to change my mindset.

Thinking back, I remember in Year 6 when we had to choose what secondary school we wanted to go to. Academic success was the last thing on my mind at that age – rather, I wanted to go to my future secondary school because I admired the older Black girls who would strut down the high street with their see-through art folders and fresh Kickers. I thought secondary school was just vibes: eating four wings and chips after school, drawing whatever you wanted in art class. Boy, was I in for a surprise. The shock of mingling with other girls who seemed much older than me as well as being in an intimidatingly large building threw me all the way off. It really was like that scene in *Mean Girls* where you're introduced to all the subcultures and cliques sitting at each table in the lunch hall. I was always somewhere in between the cool Black girls who were like family, the Bengali babes who knew how to do their make-up from early on, and the Polish girls who were into anime and showed me drawing techniques in art class.

I constantly fantasized about my future and who I would

be. My daydreams were Tracy Beaker-esque. Whenever I walked up some stairs, I'd imagine I was on my way up to a stage to accept an award. I wanted to see my name everywhere and evolve into a young woman who was just doing incredible things. I thought about it so much that it was almost like I was living that reality every time I closed my eyes. Now that I'm older, I realize I was dreaming about becoming a person who was the total opposite to me. As I type this at twenty-four years old, I think I've finally accepted who I am. I spend my days thinking about the younger me and what I would have done to change her mindset. It's like somewhere in a parallel world we're meeting in the middle and embracing. Of course, I don't want to make it seem like my entire growing-up experience was negative, but I feel that explaining all the goings-on before has helped me to realize the importance of the joy I feel within myself now and hopefully it will resonate with someone else.

After secondary school, I left for university to study media and communications, a subject I did incredibly well in without really trying. I knew I wanted to be involved in the creative industries somehow; I just wasn't sure in what capacity. There's not much to say on this chapter of my life as it was the most depressing I have endured to date. I lived in an extremely toxic household and had no money. Only three months in, I would drop out and jump on a train back home to London where I landed my first internship as a creative at an advertising agency. Four roles later – including at Nike, Ogilvy and AKQA – I had solidified my position as a young Black girl in the industry doing cool things on the side, all the while building an online presence.

On social media, I often spoke about the things I was passionate about. I loved documenting my work, other people's work I loved, my thought processes and the changes within myself as a young woman trying to navigate life. I treated my Instagram as if it were my diary, religiously logging pivotal moments in my life, right down to my first time wearing a crop top. Crop tops were something you couldn't have *paid* me to wear at one point in my life. The idea of a strip of my stomach showing made me feel sick. But, finally, I wore my first cropped hoodie to the Tate Modern. It was a solo date and the sun was out. I felt really proud of myself and posted it up. And since then, my wardrobe has been full of crop tops, bikinis, short dresses and everything else I scroll past online. Sacrificing my comfort in the name of other people's opinions is something I no longer wish to do.

Over time I built a following from my transparent captions highlighting the ups and downs of working in the creative industries and my identity as a plus-size Black girl. This core group of people who appreciated my work and values would in the future become my safe space and one of the reasons why I've been able to stay so grounded in what I do. I often spoke about my love for Peckham and my journey to finding myself and loving my body. I posted about the lack of diversity in the creative industries, which led to me taking part in speaking engagements about my experiences and work. While doing that, I was finding my place in the industry as well as finding myself as Sophia. I often posted about my thoughts and feelings towards my own body. That quickly turned into my day-to-day and I soon started following other influencers. Unfortunately, I became pretty much lost in the sauce while discovering that world.

Instagram is a cesspit of comparison and unrealistic expectations. At one point, I questioned why I was unable to afford a luxury apartment, a car and all the latest Apple products by the age of twenty-three. It sounds crazy when you say it out loud, right? But I don't blame myself for being so easily influenced when it was all I saw day in and out. The lines became blurred for me, and imposter syndrome (that feeling that tells you you're a fraud and not good enough for whatever it is you're doing) sucked the fun out of everything I did online. I wasn't sure if what I was doing or saying was right. It was a big cycle of getting to know myself, becoming lost and starting all over again.

I started to think back to that first moment when I saw somebody who looked like me and the joy I felt in that. It was all really simple and I suddenly remembered that's all it should be. I promised myself to always stay true to who I am and be proud of my background and upbringing. Over time, I've learned to ignore a lot of immediate emotions I have towards certain images. I take the time to curate my feed to make sure that I only see things and people who make me feel joy. The fat-acceptance space online has given more people the power to take ownership of their bodies – something I don't think I would have had the courage to do alone. Fat activists online have taken back the word 'fat' and simply use it as a descriptor, which is exactly what it is.

When I think of fat Black joy now, I think of my friends, some of whom I've found in the fat-acceptance space. They've each contributed to different parts of me. Some have built my confidence, some have helped me to become more emotionally intelligent, some make me laugh unprovoked, and some of them fill a void that not even family could fill. More importantly, my friends have helped me see a meaning to my existence, particularly while living in a fat body. Growing up as the fat friend, you don't really have anyone to turn to when you're feeling down. You're met with 'No, you're not fat, you're beautiful!' – as if you can't be both.

I'd like to dedicate this part to my friends Stephanie Yeboah, Enam Asiama and Vanessa Russell. These women are all plus-size and so much more than that. I didn't know what a safe space was until I met them. Not only are we all involved in the same line of work but we all share similar experiences with our bodies and can empathize with each other in a way not many other people can. Steph, Enam and Vanessa have been there for me via group chat when I'm about to board a plane and I'm texting them frantically about not being able to fit comfortably in the seat, or when I'm about to go on a date for the first time, or when I'm on set with a brand and the stylist has only picked out Size 16 clothes (which don't fit).

We are each other's security blankets, when we grew up thinking we would never have one. We laugh and joke and forget there are a few things wrong with the world. They have made me feel like everything is going to be OK and my confidence is always welcome and should never be held back.

Thanks to these women and so many others, I am truly at a place where I feel joy in being myself, existing online and in the real world as a plus-size Black girl doing *bits*.

FIND YOUR OWN JOY

Take a picture of yourself in an item of clothing you've always been a bit apprehensive about. Go the extra mile and post it online!

Fat activists online have taken back the word 'fat' and simply use it as a descriptor, which is exactly what it is

We Didn't Need a Village

On being raised on an estate

Ife Grillo

PRODUCER, WRITER, CAMPAIGNER,
PERFORMER & EDUCATOR

Illustration by Emma Hall

Every Saturday, when I'd come home from drama class, I'd be locked out because my parents had gone to Hoxton Street Market. I'd go through the market trying to find them, and eventually, whenever the traders saw me, they would just point me to where they were, which was usually buying clothes that could eventually be given to 'someone back home' in Nigeria.

An east London marketplace is the best pantomime that exists. Every Saturday morning the estate woke up and got ready to give a showstopping performance. I got to see women from my estate put on their best face, command a stage and sell Fruit of the Loom T-shirts like they were Versace. I heard bossmen sing their choruses, telling tales of affordable fruit and veg like they were stars in a West End musical. I watched the aunties sit outside their shopfronts and offer free sweets and prayers to children who were carrying more shopping bags than their arms gave them strength for. More than anything, I listened. I listened to what it sounds like when people come together to create a sense of community in a world that doesn't tend to make space for it. I witnessed what it looks like when an estate does what it is meant to do and creates connections between those who would otherwise be strangers. I'm not here to tell you that living on an estate is always a perfect dreamland; like all family structures, there are issues. However, in a society that can be very isolating, estates create an avenue for community living, and that shouldn't be looked over.

Estates and social housing have been part of the UK for over a hundred years. In 1919, as a response to the devastations of the war, Parliament passed the Housing and Town Planning Act to subsidize the construction of houses for people. As the years passed, many Black migrants settled into estates in cities such as London, Bristol and Manchester, and in 2016 it was found that nearly half of all Black British people in the UK still lived in social housing.

The great thing about living on an estate is getting to connect with such a wide range of people. When I was younger, I didn't need to take an exploratory trip across the globe, because within my neighbourhood we hosted the world. Even though we weren't running cultural exhibitions, I learned so much about the cultures that shaped my area.

One of my favourite memories is of my Turkish neighbour giving me some sweets to try after hearing me complain that Turkish delight wasn't as good as they'd made it out to be in the Narnia films. It was a small act that in the grand scheme of things shouldn't have mattered, but I felt like I had been personally gifted a delicacy by the Turkish ambassador. The people on my estate helped me understand what it meant to be proud of one's culture and wear it with honour while still embracing and celebrating difference. Hackney has always

" When I was younger, I didn't need to take an exploratory trip across the globe, because **within my neighbourhood we hosted the world "**

been a tapestry of different communities trying to find a home. Estate life forces you to be in each other's faces and appreciate what each other can bring.

Outside of cultural differences, estate living allowed me to connect with people I would never have engaged with otherwise. Most of us don't tend to connect with elderly people outside of our family. I'm thankful that my estate allowed me to have genuine conversations with those born long before me who had knowledge, and treats, to share. It meant I got to appreciate them as strong, multi-dimensional individuals instead of just seeing them as elderly. Also, when I look back, I realize that I only knew certain jobs existed because of people on my estate. Whether it was speaking to someone who worked in the NHS or learning about what it took to run your own business, living on an estate was like having a careers fair on your doorstep. It helped remind me that, even through struggle, many different types of life exist.

I also loved being constantly surrounded by other young people. I didn't grow up with a huge bag of cousins, so the kids on my estate made me feel like I was never short on company. Making friends is never easy but having a shared sense of place made it easier to form bonds and find my people. In a world before social media and smartphones, someone 'knocking for you' was worth more than a Blue Peter badge. I still remember that feeling of anticipation when my

Emma Hall

brother's and my friends would ring our buzzer and we'd race to the door so we could answer it before our parents. With our chores done and our arguments prepared, we'd make our case for being allowed out as if our parents were government ministers granting us citizenship. If we were lucky enough to get a yes then we'd leave knowing we had to be out all day, because the moment we set foot back in our flat we weren't leaving again. Like the Pied Piper, we'd go round, block by block, collecting other kids as we avalanched towards the playground.

Looking back, I can confidently say that no one has more fun than an estate kid on a long summer's day. While our playground facilities may have been simple, with just the football cage, swing set and slide, it was pretty magical: a place you felt you had some ownership over, and that no one could take from you. I remember matches on the estate football pitch feeling like Premier League finals, and big games of hide-and-seek revealing secrets and creating lovers among the clan. When I think about how much fun I used to have, I am reminded that, for young me, true friendship and camaraderie were found playing knock-down-ginger and buying 15p ice lollies. Most who live on estates don't have a lot of money to spend on holidays and presents, so we learned how to make our own adventures. We taught ourselves how to make a six-week summer feel like a montage in an American coming-of-age movie, and we got to properly appreciate the hidden power of play. Even the simple act of having a group of people to walk to and from school with made me feel more willing to take on the day. As kids of the estate, we looked out for each other and protected our own. We learned that there is strength and power in numbers and the importance of having someone's back. We came together with a shared sense of imagination and created a metropolitan kingdom for ourselves.

That's the thing with living on an estate: whether as children or as adults, we watched out for each other. In the years since I left, I have never seen selflessness the way I did growing up. Many of my best clothes were hand-me-downs from my neighbour who lived on the floor below us. She would drop bags of clothes that didn't fit her boys any more at our house and never expect anything back. We never asked for them, but she gave them anyway. It was because of her kindness that I had football trainers that I loved, and it was because of her generosity that non-uniform day felt like my runway debut instead of being a strain on my parents' finances. For better or worse, we all know that how you dress as a child has a huge impact on how you're treated by your peers. Maybe my neighbour wanted to protect me from that, or maybe she just thought it would be useful for us, but either way she helped me feel confident.

" As kids of the estate, we looked out for each other and protected our own. **We learned that there is strength and power in numbers and the importance of having someone's back** "

She wasn't the only generous neighbour though: the person who taught me how to ride a bike was also a guy on my estate. He had no real connection to my family and didn't even live in my building, but he taught me with all of the love and patience that a father has for their son. I was a terrible learner and got very frustrated any time I fell, but he persisted and made me feel like I could do it. When I finally started pedalling around the corner of my estate, I wasn't just happy that I could go bike-riding with my friends – I was happy because I knew he'd be proud.

I could think of countless others who showed me kindness on the estate, but those two will always stick out in my mind because they were so casual with their generosity. They never made it a big thing; it was like they just did it instinctively. If you asked me now, I couldn't tell you either of their names. I don't even properly remember what they look like. All I can remember is that they were kind to me, without wanting anything in return. When people ask me where my sense of community comes from, I know it was partly birthed in those moments. That's another thing I loved about estate living: people understood that everyone was just trying their best to get through life and look after their family. That shared respect and understanding underpinned every action. We all knew that the world wasn't easy or made for people like us, so we helped and found community in each other. We showed up for each other but knew when to mind our business. People shared skills and resources when they didn't have to because they felt part of a bigger family. Even though I was young, that sense of duty to those around me shaped me. It taught me that you should never feel like you have to wait until you've 'made it' to start giving back. In a world where everyone feels the need to monetize everything, estate living is a sharp reminder that small selfless acts can make huge impacts on people's lives, and not everything needs to be about your own growth.

My favourite thing about my estate was that we didn't just work together – we felt proud doing it. We took pride in our area and wore our I ♥ Hackney badges like they were diamond brooches. When summer bloomed and it was time for Hackney Carnival, we'd put on our best clothes and dance like we were headlining Wireless. I remember working on a project with the kids in my area where we made mosaics that were going to be put up in the new park. From the look on my face, you'd have thought I was painting the next *Mona Lisa*. I spent days on my mosaic, and when it was finished and I got to see it for the first time, I felt a special type of pride. Celebrating my local area and making it more beautiful gave me a sense of purpose. It allowed me to shape my sense of belonging as opposed to it being shaped for me. As I had more and more of those moments, I started to understand the extent to which being proud of my estate and Hackney was part of my identity.

When I was young, I remember feeling so defensive when I talked about Hackney and the estate I lived on. It was as if I'd get ready to defend my home town like my life depended on it before the other person had even said anything. As I got older, I started to ask myself why it was so important to me to defend my estate's honour. What it was about the place that made me so passionate and loyal. That's the thing about growing up in an area like that: it sneaks up on you. I knew the people were great, and I loved how dynamic the area felt, but as I got older I began to properly appreciate how important my sense of place was to my understanding of who I was. It's hard to separate the areas where we grew up from how we see ourselves today. Eventually, many of us get so invested in our area that we want to take bigger steps to look after it. It was my pride in Hackney that ultimately led me to get involved in community work and organizing. While not everyone goes down that route, I know a lot of people who first got fired up politically because of the area they grew up in. When parks were messy and not fit for purpose, the locals came together to demand better. When community organizations needed money, people ran fundraising drives and gave up their time. When you've grown up on an estate, and in a community that's used to not getting the chance to be seen, it's miraculous seeing the impact people can make when something matters to them. Every time I got to witness people fight for the place they loved, it gave me permission to take up space.

It's hard to summarize what growing up on an estate did for me. It showed me a small example of what it means to feel community in Britain. Being a Nigerian, I've always understood that family extends beyond the home. It's ingrained in our culture to build communities and create kin, and whenever I'm around Nigerians I know I'm in the presence of family, even if it is the first time we've ever met. I feel that way around most Black British people. Even if we have little in common, we know how to give each other a look that says, 'I see you, you're valid, good luck.' However, estates allowed me to access a broader sense of community, which Black British people are often denied. I don't want to romanticize the difficulties that can exist when you grow up on an estate – but the sense of togetherness they can create is a lesson that the UK needs to learn, and I'm thankful I got to experience it.

In our little microcosm of society, we created a world where sometimes you could just let go. We lived off resilience but also laughter and warmth. We helped each other without question or motive, and we found ways to keep things going and fight for what we thought was important. Ultimately, we knew that coming together gave us strength, so we learned how to compromise and be part of the team.

Honestly, I am still slightly annoyed about the number of Saturday afternoons I spent rushing around the market, looking for my mum and dad. Sometimes I found them almost instantly, and other times it took a while. Either way, wherever I looked, I saw many familiar faces smiling at me. Regardless of how long it would take me to find my parents, I knew I was already home.

FIND YOUR OWN JOY

Write down three instances where someone in your neighbourhood has shown you an act of kindness.

Embracing the Absurd

How my existential nihilism became joyful

Rukiat Ashawe

SEX EDUCATOR, WRITER
& CONTENT CREATOR

WARNING: this essay discusses suicidal thoughts
and feelings which some readers may find upsetting
or triggering.

Existential nihilism is the rather scary philosophical theory that life has no intrinsic meaning or value. There is no grand or significant reason as to why we are here. We just are. This belief can cause you to feel resentment towards the world for its faults and for the fact that you were born into it. You end up having trouble seeing the good in anything and prefer to wallow in self-pity as you come to terms with the fact that you are not special. You are not here for some divine purpose and there is no outside force orchestrating your life. You are truly left to your own devices, and that can feel terrifying.

As a Black British person, finding joy in nihilism has been difficult. When so much emphasis is placed on your identity from the world around you, the emptiness that nihilism causes within can feel contradictory. From society telling me who I needed to be as a Black person, that my Blackness meant that I will always face hardship, to my Nigerian culture placing so much importance on religion and destiny, having these nihilistic thoughts almost felt like a betrayal.

Like most people who were raised by Nigerian immigrant parents in the UK, religion was at the centre of my culture. My dad was, and still is, a devout Muslim man. From early on in my childhood he would insist that I attended Islamic lessons to study the Quran. I didn't resist his wishes at first; in fact, I embraced Islam and would get into fervent discussions with my Christian friends at primary school over which religion was right, whether Jesus was truly the son of God, and our own notions of heaven and hell. I was passionate and would defend Islam with every cell within me, determined to win the frequent arguments we had during our lunch breaks.

But by the time I had reached my teens, my beliefs took an unexpected turn. A reluctant trip to the church with my mum and aunty ended in me suddenly giving my life to Christ. I don't remember what the pastor said that night but it resonated with me and so I was 'saved'. This was the purpose of my life, the path that I was meant to take. It took a while for my dad to find out as he never lived with us, but when he did, he was upset about my new choice of religion. Nonetheless, I stood my ground as I was so sure that Jesus, the son of God, was my saviour and that I had found fulfilment in my servitude to him.

It all seemed to make perfect sense. My life had meaning and value. I found purpose and joy through a belief system, and a hope was instilled within me that one day I would be free from this life, this sinful and wretched world we call planet Earth. Jesus Christ was waiting for me on the other side and I looked forward to spending an infinite, eternal bliss with him in the New Jerusalem. Not to mention that with Christianity came a sense of community through my church. The members felt like family and they were mostly

Nigerian and Black British, so my connection with them was intrinsically linked to my identity.

I have always been inquisitive in nature, and I have a deep interest in the future. So much so that when I first converted to Christianity I read the Book of Revelation over and over. The end times, the apocalypse, Armageddon – the concept of a destructive and tragic end to mankind was so intriguing to me that I became fully invested in it. I would spend hours as a young teen searching the internet for answers, ordering free books, listening to sermons and audiotapes, and watching YouTube videos. I fell into a dark hole that led me to believe that cults ran the world and they had plans for a New World Order. This was during the mid-2000s, when the internet was a different place and it was arguably much easier to fall for conspiracy theories and fake news.

Now when I think about it, I wonder what a fourteen-year-old was doing spending her time researching dark theories about the future. Why did I care so much? At that age, the prospect of a bitter finale shouldn't have mattered to me; it should never have even crossed my mind. But it did, and not only was I consumed by it but the thought excited me. You might expect that the realization of a devastating end would leave me feeling hopeless and lost, and questions like 'What is the point of it all?' would be running through my mind. Instead, I felt joyful because I believed that after the end would come the future that had been promised to me by my religion.

Even though I was inquisitive, my quest for more was within the confinements of my own personal ignorance because I was still beholden to religion. Its glass walls had not yet begun to crack. This is not to say that believing in a religion makes you ignorant, but during that period of my life my eyes and my mind were clouded. And I don't think that ignorance is always a bad thing. It is like a safety net sometimes: it gives you security, shields you from the unknown. Ignorance allows you to live within a bubble and to go about your merry day, never questioning why things are the way they are, but instead accepting what you are told.

It was social justice and science fiction that disrupted everything. I was at the start of my twenties, in my first year of university. Many 'social justice warriors' will tell you that they were the loudest, most passionate and most obsessive at the start of their journeys – I was too. As a Black person, once you swallow the red pill of social justice, you learn more about intersectionality and various axes of power that affect Black people, such as institutional racism and white supremacy. The red pill wakes you up to a matrix of oppression that you never fully grasped. You now have this raging fire within you to fight for what is right, to abolish the system that keeps you mentally enslaved. And if you upheld a different set of beliefs prior to becoming a social justice warrior, religions like Christianity often become the 'white man's religion' that you must free yourself from.

I stopped believing in Jesus and became distant from my church community. I had several arguments with my mother about my departure from the religion. I even had dreams that I was kicked out of church and ostracized not only from my community but from the world itself. Losing that connection was devastating, but social justice made me feel like I was connecting with my Blackness in a new way. In many ways I was, but mostly what it did was change my perception of my Black identity. Being Black now felt like I was fighting oppression every day, like the world was constantly against me, and when I look back to that period in my life I see it wasn't healthy. There is no joy in walking through the world every day with that mindset.

Alongside my interest in social justice, I had a growing love for cyberpunk, a subculture and genre of science fiction that imagines bleak and dystopian visions of the future. Usually the story is set in a neo-noir, technologically advanced city where corporations rule the masses and there are only two classes: the elites and everybody else. Other times it depicts a post-apocalyptic future where the rapid advancement of artificial intelligence or a deadly man-made virus has led to the collapse of society. Movies like the Matrix trilogy, *The*

Animatrix, Ultraviolet, Terminator, Ex Machina, Equilibrium, A.I. Artificial Intelligence and *I, Robot* and video games like *Mirror's Edge* had a profound effect on my life and changed my world view yet again. Even though they were science fiction, the ideas that they presented were not too far-fetched.

Unfortunately, having left religion behind, I was now in deep despair by these new discoveries. This was because not only was I experiencing a disillusionment about Christianity but also ideas like 'nothing matters' began to encroach on my thoughts. I was gradually adopting a very nihilistic view of the future that was devoid of any messiah coming to save me on a white horse before the world ended. Nothing was worth fighting or living for in my eyes. I felt crippling feelings of sadness and hopelessness. The question 'What is the point of it all?' suddenly became all I could think about. What made it worse was that around this time I was also failing so badly at my studies. I felt incredibly lonely as a student and my confidence was at an all-time low. I found it difficult to be happy or find the motivation to do anything.

I decided to ignore these feelings, rather than face them head-on, and just get on with life. Rather than confront my existential nihilist thoughts, I put them to the back of my mind and faked optimism. I continued to do that through my interest in social justice. By clinging to the idea of overthrowing patriarchy, racism, gender binaries and capitalism, I feigned hope. By clinging on to the prospect of an equal future, I could continue to survive, continue to stay out of the dark corners of my mind and continue to live in the present. But deep down in my heart, these were fallacies to me. Lies that I had convinced myself to believe, even though they were far from what I considered to be the truth.

I have learned that this coping mechanism actually has a name: philosophical suicide. You see, these internal dilemmas that I battled within myself were nothing new. Feelings of dread and pessimism and the idea that we are all doomed can be found on the Reddit and Twitter spheres of millennials and Gen Z, and in the works of great thinkers of the past who shared with the world their own feelings of doom and gloom.

The French writer and thinker Albert Camus sought to find solutions to deal with existential nihilism and developed the philosophy of absurdism. The absurd, according to Camus, is the contradiction of humans endlessly trying to find meaning in a world that is inherently meaningless, and he proposed three ways to deal with it.

The first is suicide. I've never spoken about this publicly before, but this was something that I seriously considered during my most depressive episodes. There were several times that I felt suicidal and believed that the only way to escape this emptiness was to take my own life. But I never had the courage to go through with it and so here I am.

The second was what I mentioned earlier: philosophical suicide, meaning that one would have to choose faith over rationality and logic. Usually this would be in the form of a religion or a spiritual-based system. In a way, it's kind of like pretending that your life has meaning in order to alleviate yourself from the hollowness that the meaningless of your existence brings. This can also come in the form of pretending to fight for a cause you believe in, even though deep down you know that it all means nothing in the end. This is what I did for a very long time. This was my way of coping until last year when I discovered the third way of dealing with the absurd: acceptance.

To accept the absurd is to choose life despite its nothingness. This solution was the one that Camus pushed for the most and one that I agree with. I've heard other young people use terms such as 'sunny nihilism', 'positive nihilism' and 'optimistic nihilism', all of which accept that human existence has no underlying meaning and that this premise should be taken as a positive reality. At first glance, it sounds like a confusing way to live. How could anybody find happiness in such a mindset? Especially in our current times where Black people are louder than ever and collectively believe that they must stand up for something. That our identities must always be political, always centre on fighting for equality. To be Black is to be purpose-led. But accepting the absurd for me was rejecting the idea of purpose and the burdens that come with it, especially during a period of time where it felt like society was collapsing all around me. Embracing the absurd was the most freeing feeling. I felt relieved. Like pressure had been lifted off my shoulders as my search for some sort of enlightenment, for something greater outside of myself, was put to rest.

The sense of relief reminded me of a brilliant short story called 'Zima Blue' from the *Life, Death and Robots* series on Netflix. 'Zima Blue' is about a robot that was designed to clean pools but goes through several modifications to the point where it becomes self-aware, like a human. With this self-awareness comes a quest to find its purpose in the universe. And so this robot travels the cosmos and seeks more modifications to enhance its search for something more. In the end, the robot concludes that there is no great purpose and instead chooses to let go of exceptionalism. It also decides to remove the modifications and go back to living as a simple machine that cleans pools.

Although I have no simple version of myself to resort back to because I believe that I was born without purpose, I still found comfort in this story. I don't need some grandiose justification for my existence; I simply exist. I don't need to feel helpless at the thought of humans eventually meeting a bleak ending, because no life form lasts forever – and they're

"Embracing the absurd was the most freeing feeling. I felt relieved. Like pressure had been lifted off my shoulders **as my search for some sort of enlightenment, for something greater outside of myself, was put to rest**" not supposed to. We are not immortals; the world does not revolve around us. We are merely blips in this vast amount of space that we call the universe.

I don't need my identity to revolve around pain and suffering either. Saying this is not denying the various systems of power that need to oppress marginalized individuals in order to survive. But what many people don't realize is that letting go of the pain is an act of resistance. Black people should be allowed to choose not to stand up for anything or believe in something without being penalized for it. Black people should be allowed to seek out the simple pleasures of life, to get what they can out of it while they are here. To make the most out of the present, to not worry about the future, to not constantly live on the edge. Not every Black person should be expected to fight or believe in the fight itself.

In my opinion, whether it all ends tragically or beautifully should not have such an influence on the quality of my life. In the end, nothing really matters anyways, so why wallow in a pool of anguish and misery? Why focus on the negatives that have done nothing but drive me further into an abyss? Unfortunately, one cannot survive in this world without succumbing to the work ethic of our capitalist society. But it is possible to find balance despite the need to ensure your survival. Balance for me is being able to indulge in the simple things that bring me joy, such as fashion and cosplay. And being able to rest and look after myself. And, of course, not taking life too seriously.

That is my conclusion for now, and, based on the journey that I have told you so far, it is very much subject to change. And there is nothing wrong with that. Change is what comes from new life experiences, from reading books, from meeting new people, from travelling, from growing older. Change is unavoidable. But where I am at now mentally has given me so much peace, so much freedom. How radical is it to find such harmony in the midst of a pandemic? While the world around me was chaotic and unpredictable, somehow I managed to find a middle ground. I managed to make sense of my existence by finding the courage to accept it for what it is and rejecting the notions of my identity that have been forced upon me.

I don't have life all figured out, nor will I ever have all the answers, but I am content with that matter of fact. And not only am I content, but this level of understanding I have of myself brings me so much joy.

FIND YOUR OWN JOY

Watch 'Zima Blue' from *Love, Death and Robots* on Netflix. It will help you understand my essay better and will make you think about life, its meaning and your purpose.

"Balance for me is being able to indulge in the simple things that bring me joy, such as fashion and cosplay. **And being able to rest and look after myself. And, of course, not taking life too seriously**"

Euphoric Escapism
A question
of sport

Mayowa Quadri
BRAND AND EDITORIAL OFFICER FOR VERSUS

'Why aren't you studying instead of running around?'

If, like me, you were an active kid, you will have been asked this question many times by nosy aunties and strict uncles. I have been accused of focusing too much on sport more times than I can count. But to reduce it to 'running around'? That running around has helped me in ways people could not imagine. Why would a form of enjoyment be seen as a distraction? It's something I've never been able to get my head around. Growing up, people saw what I was doing with sport instead of what sport was doing *for* me. Perhaps they didn't understand what I was trying to escape.

As a young Black boy growing up in south-east London, my adolescence was filled with moments where I felt intense pressure socially, economically and culturally. I recall my friendship groups changing rapidly as I saw people head down the wrong path. When you live in an area where gang culture resides, it's very easy to fall into that lifestyle. Some people end up in those circles due to peer pressure; others due to poverty.

Fortunately, I had sport, which kept me away from things that could have drawn me into a downward spiral. I've been involved in sport for as long as I can remember, especially football and athletics. From the age of five, I was dropped at after-school clubs and holiday camps, and soon I began to represent my school at football, athletics and basketball tournaments. When I got older, I played football in professional environments and coached the local team.

Sport wasn't just about entertainment for me. It always served as an escape. Each day of the week when I was growing up, I had reason to be away from certain places and people. Monday through to Sunday, you couldn't find me – I was at training or games. I got to travel, meet new people and learn more about myself before having to return to my 'reality'.

Despite being bright and possessing 'all the potential in the world' (a phrase often repeated by teachers at parents' evenings), there were times in school where I lost interest. The curriculum was not tailored to people who were expressive and learned through channelling their energy into sport or art, and I often felt restricted. Nothing I was learning felt real. I would sit through history lessons on the Second World War and struggle to apply them to real life; in maths, I was sure that Pythagoras's theorem was important but couldn't work out when I would have to use it. I felt any progress I made academically wasn't celebrated. The vibes in the classroom with friends were great, but the actual learning wasn't. Sport helped me overcome boredom. Without it, my grades probably would have plummeted.

Even today, whether I'm playing in an eleven-a-side match or watching *Match of the Day*, nothing else matters for that period of time. Sport takes priority. I think back to school and the feeling of joy knowing that lunchtime was fast approaching. As soon as the bell would sound, I would be on the pitch in a flash. For one hour, I could forget about coursework due in and just enjoy myself. It could have been playing football in Kickers with the smallest goals you've ever seen, patball against a battered wall or basketball with the slanted hoop and ripped net – that one hour allowed me to be free because I was having fun with my friends.

As well as sport allowing me to get away from my troubles, in all honesty I also saw it as my pathway into the 'big league'. At one point, I had dreams of competing in football and athletics at the same time. Wild, I know. The narrative that sport is a ticket to changing your family's destiny financially may be well worn, but that doesn't make it any less of a genuine dream for many young people. I saw myself as someone who had more ability than most, and the luxurious lifestyles of professional athletes like Ashley Cole fascinated and motivated me. I wanted my fair share.

Raising a young boy as a single parent is not easy, and I remember days when my mum would work overtime to make sure she could pay the bills and give me enough money for school, even if it meant she didn't have much for herself. I would occasionally get some small change from selling Capri-Sun and jam doughnuts from Sainsbury's to my peers and would give the cash to my mum, but it was nowhere near enough to help in the long term. And, to be frank, although

On the field, we were equals. In those moments, I and other young Black boys, regardless of where we were from, had a common ground it was taken as a sweet gesture, it probably broke her heart. Not being able to help her broke mine. To me, it felt like sport could change everything.

Many of us have had these same aspirations. I have friends in their mid-twenties who play semi-professional football and are still holding out for that last window of opportunity. It reminds me of the over-25s group in *The X Factor* – a few may defy the odds and achieve the 'impossible' dream, but the reality is that less than 0.012% of football players make it to the Premier League. And when it comes to sport in general, not all of us can be professionals or experience the riches of celebrity. On the flip side, just because we don't make it to the 'top spot' or earn big money doesn't mean sport can't be useful to us.

One of the greatest things sport has given me is the ability to create memories with amazing people. I've had team-mates whom I would never have spoken to outside of football because they were from parts of the city that were considered forbidden areas. In a time of postcode rivalry, your school blazer indicated where you came from – and let's just say it wasn't a good idea to walk in certain places alone. But on the field, we were equals. In those moments, I and other young Black boys, regardless of where we were from, had a common ground.

Six-week summer holidays on the estate were spent

kicking a ball around for hours on end and climbing over fences to use the goals in local primary schools. It feels like just yesterday, no cares in the world, young and free. It didn't matter if an older in the area kicked our ball over a roof and we had to risk our life getting it down – we were just happy to be playing. We loved football and we didn't want to go home. Make the mistake of popping indoors for a glass of water and you might not see your friends till tomorrow: there was something about going and coming that used to frustrate our parents – you either stayed at home or stayed outside. Even in this, there was a life lesson: enjoy everything while you can. Those moments of camaraderie were golden.

The harsher side to sport is, of course, the competition. But, growing up, even that could be exciting. School sports days were hard to top. Being the best in the class in a subject is cool, but you don't usually get to publicly prove your prowess in science or English. For a football and athletics prodigy like myself, there was sports day. Our teachers were the broadcasters, our friends were the fans, and we were the superstars.

One of my best friends, Ibrahim, was my fiercest competitor. We raced at school and track meets. I often remind him how lucky he was to beat me in our last ever race. It was the Year 10 sports day. A rivalry that had gone on for four years ended in heartbreak for me and jubilation for him. In the 4x100m relay, he had the better team, yet he only *just* beat me in our battle on the home straight. If the track had been 10 metres longer, I would have smoked him. He often tells me that I'm just bitter.

Of course, everyone loves winning, but we can learn from moments of 'failure' too. My greatest memories aren't of the victories – I value the journey and experience so much more. As Black people, we face challenges in our everyday lives: to be the best academically, to work harder than our white counterparts, to be better than our parents, to be examples for the next generation, to change the narrative. In this chase for perfection, we may fall short. Things may not go how we want them to go. But that's OK. Success is not purely defined by winning. It's how you turn losses into wins. How you come back from hitting rock bottom. I often reiterate to the young people I coach that being goal-orientated is great, but what was learned in the process?

One of my greatest sporting moments was finally getting into the academy of a professional football team in Luton. It felt like it had taken a lifetime, but at the age of fifteen I finally had success at a trial. Three of my friends also took part in the trial: Denzel, Stefan and, of course, Ibrahim. This time, I got the upper hand over my arch-nemesis. In fact, just three people out of seventy were called back and I was the only one from my group of friends to make the cut. This achievement

"Success is not purely defined by winning. **It's how you turn losses into wins.** How you come back from hitting rock bottom " was momentous for me, and it would have been easy to get caught up in the moment and presume that I was going to go on to become a professional, leaving my friends behind. But the biggest lesson I learned was the value of real friendships. None of my friends were bitter and their support gave me the fire to make sure I made the most out of the experience.

Based on everything I have said until this point, you're probably wondering: *Why isn't this guy a professional now?* The truth is that other factors come into whether you make it to the top. Luck, injuries, timing, perceptions of coaches, family support, you name it. Remember that dream I had of doing both football and athletics? Turns out it wasn't quite possible.

Each sport requires full dedication, and during a difficult summer I had to make a decision between the two sports I loved. As much as I was in awe of Olympians and the thrill of racing, there was just something about football. The thrill of beating an opponent, working as a team to achieve a common objective, seeing that pass that no one else could see, the euphoria of scoring a winning goal, the jubilation and celebrations, even the feeling of revenge after you'd received a horrible tackle. I chose my Luton trial instead of spending the summer training for track meets. I chose the one I loved more rather than the one I was slightly better at.

But, despite Luton being a great moment, I realized for the first time that being good was not good enough. I worked as the opening ceremony. My mind was blown. Not only could you be crowned the best in the world, but you could also be crowned on your own turf. More heroes were born for me that summer. Jessica Ennis became women's heptathlon champion on 'Super Saturday', the same day Mo Farah would win the first of his two gold medals. We also had Anthony Joshua and Nicola Adams who were victorious in boxing. Greatness. AJ's victory in particular hit home. Like me, he is a Nigerian Brit. Like people I knew, he'd got himself into some trouble. Like for me, sport was a form of escapism that allowed him to get away from the wrong crowd and change the direction his life was heading in.

Despite not making it professional, I have an abundance of life skills that have helped me to this day. Sport may not have brought me fame and riches, but it taught me leadership and teamwork. I gained independence from my late-night journeys to and from Luton by myself. I learned how to prioritize by knowing that I couldn't attend training if I didn't finish my homework. Sport developed me. I love nothing more than going on a run when the pressures of the world get too much. And I can break the awkward silence in an office just by asking what team everyone supports. That's what I find most important.

This may differ for others. Your escapism could be arts and crafts, gaming or baking. It may not always make you money, but it can free you from the daily stresses you face.

hard as I could, but injuries caught up with me. My desire to study while playing led me into a lower standard of football while in college and the resounding feeling that maybe I would not be part of that 0.012%. Ultimately, it wasn't meant to be.

A drawn-out narrative is that the only way to make it in life as a young Black person is by going into music or sport. Black British writer Derek A. Bardowell explored this notion in his book *No Win Race: A Story of Belonging, Britishness and Sport*, writing: 'It had often been the case that white people assumed that the colour of my skin and my height ensured athletic excellence.' Thinking back to my own experiences, I remember times when PE teachers would say the Black boys ran quicker times because of our 'natural fast-twitch muscles'. Such statements and beliefs are dangerous, in my opinion. It discredits the efforts of Black athletes and purely praises genetics while also fuelling this practice of pushing Black kids into sports. 'Naturally gifted' is what they call it. On the flip side, white counterparts will play sports that are deemed to need a higher skill level or IQ. Essentially, it's discriminatory and limiting. Fortunately, things are changing now and we have various examples of great Black people breaking down doors in industries outside of music and sport – whether as writers, content creators, fashion designers, software developers, podiatrists or construction managers. We now know that the world is truly our oyster.

My drive to make it as a professional was also because I wanted to be like my role models. Representation plays a massive part in the decisions we make in life. The fact that there were Black people on my TV screen who looked like me, spoke like me and had a similar upbringing to me was inspirational and provided a blueprint for me to follow. I had many idols who are Black British greats. People like footballer Jermain Defoe, who played for Spurs and was mentioned in Bashy's 2007 song dedicated to Black boys. Closer to home, there was Rio Ferdinand, who grew up in Peckham – literally down the road from me. I saw him achieve some of the biggest accolades in the game: Champions League winner, Premier League winner and England captain. It's crazy because if he was younger, there could have been a real chance that he and I would have played football on the estate. He was everything I wanted to be in life, and his unapologetic realness in the media made him even more relatable.

My other role models were Olympians. I was nine years old when I witnessed Kelly Holmes bring home two gold medals from the Athens Olympics in 2004, alongside an all-Black British quartet of Darren Campbell, Marlon Devonish, Jason Gardener and Mark Lewis-Francis who won gold in the men's 4x100m relay. Fast-forward to the London Olympics in 2012. A home Olympics. The greatest stars in the world were on my doorstep and I was fortunate enough to go to

Not becoming your idols doesn't mean you can't emulate them. I still try to channel Rio when I play football. I treat my local five-a-side like a World Cup final. I may not get the massive crowd that the pros get, but the mandem cheering is enough for me. If you partake in sports and have aspirations, that's great. You may not achieve them all, or the destination you end up in may not be what you thought it would be, but, believe me, you will realize there was a reason for that and find a blessing in it. Ultimately, why you take part in sport is the most important thing. And, for me, it has always been and always will be a pathway to joy.

FIND YOUR OWN JOY

Have a look around your house for anything that reminds you of sport when you were younger. It could be your first-place medal from football, your Stage 3 swimming certificate or even pictures of you in a sports kit. If you have nothing in physical form, think of the first sporting memory that comes to mind and hold on to it. (If it is your family members watching a match on the TV, this is perfectly normal!)

Jaiye Jaiye, Faaji Faaji

The delight of Nigerian hall parties

Tobi Kyeremateng

PRODUCER & WRITER

Saturdays belonged to D Boss. On any given weekend, you would find him traipsing up and down his block, all bald-headed and proud-postured, donning a pair of sunglasses whatever the weather. A gold pendant hung nobly from a chain around his neck, swinging side to side and catching the sunlight – almost as if it were winking back at the sky – as he would grace each of his neighbours' front doors with a wide grin and open invitation. *Five doors to the right, five doors to the left, down to the floor below and repeat until all twenty-one homes have received a personal invite.* An invitation to one of D Boss's parties wasn't to be taken lightly: they were flamboyant, thoroughly planned occasions that, like most Nigerian 'indoor parties' (house parties) and 'outdoor parties' (hall parties or owambe), required a resilient liver, the stamina of a long-distance runner and light feet for endless dancing. There was a particular pride to be taken in hosting parties, especially 'Why not?' parties that didn't call for any specific occasion to circle its way back around the sun. 'People say we Nigerians take parties too seriously – and yes, we do!' D Boss would say, punctuating the air with a nod in agreement with himself. 'It's part of our tradition. Parties are never forgotten.' And at the end of each party, it was always confirmed: if there was anyone who knew how to host, it was D Boss.

D Boss is a social man, and it wasn't until my late teens that I discovered his real name. It isn't unusual for elders to be christened with titles that reflect aspects of their personalities, and 'Uncle Manny' didn't feel as fitting an alias. D Boss, being someone who revelled in carving out spaces to party wherever he landed, considered hosting to be a refined art form, and being a good host was a badge of honour he flaunted in all his unwavering Nigerian pride. 'I've hosted parties all over: Bolton, Elephant and Castle, Edmonton, East Ham, on boats, in all the houses I have lived in and all the halls I could afford to hire,' he tells me on the other end of our phone call.

My christening into Nigerian party traditions took place in D Boss's house in the early 2000s, watching his tall, pot-bellied figure jollying up and down as he laughed heartily. Glee radiated from him and buried itself into the soul of his parties, and when the weekend would come and Mum would say, 'We're going to D Boss's,' the unspoken anticipation would rattle around the house like the feeling you get on Christmas Eve. Mum isn't much of a partygoer, but she would describe the time she spent living with D Boss when she first moved to London in the early 1990s as 'every day feeling like a party', with guests passing through to say hello and ending up staying until the morning birds called them home. 'Once it starts, oh my goodness, you won't want to leave,' she tells me. 'I always had a good time. At the end, I always thought, "I could do this again!"' – and she would.

My earliest memories of these parties are distinct. The

familiar scents of hard liquor and spiced foods carry me towards the kitchen. In the corner of my eye is a blue bucket full of ice moving like Tetris, cradling bobbing bottles of Supermalt and cans of Lilt. Back then, Supermalt was the elixir of life – a delicacy only brought out at Christmas and birthdays and ferried home in abundance after parties. Nobody prepared me for the fact that Supermalt was essentially a meal in a bottle, and at every party I would crack one open and attempt to glug it down with the unfiltered audacity most children have, soon realizing that my stomach wouldn't be able to hold both the malt and the unsupervised overflow of sweet chin-chin.

As soon as you arrived, the aunties would say, 'Oya, go and play with your cousins!' – as if they had been waiting for the moment they could drop their shoulders and just be – and off you went with a group of children who you weren't sure were your actual cousins or just the children of the elders.

Like a thrown-together pop group, all of us children would sneak downstairs away from the 'children's party', only to be stopped dead in our tracks. 'Oluwatobi! Bawo ni? Ah, you don't remember me?' – the calling card of miscellaneous aunties everywhere who 'used to bath you as a baby' or 'visited your mum when you were born'. I'd dobale and exchange nervous smiles with the aunty, who I wasn't sure was an actual aunty or just an elder, while watching my maybe-cousins shovel spoonfuls of jollof and ripe plantain into their mouths.

When the clock would announce that too much time – yet not enough time at all – had passed, we would sleepily zombie-walk ourselves back to Mum's car, her headwrap unravelling as a sign of a good night, stacking crates of food and drink into the boot that would last us until the next party. The drive back was in a silence full of pleasure: the intermittent snigger from Mum and Dad as they both sat lost in their memories; the snore from my brother as he dribbled his dreams on to his waistcoat; the glaring lights of a London night blurring into a frenzy while Capital FM murmured a techno song through the radio to remind us of our Britishness. My favourite part of the evening came with a rocking motion, swaying back and forth with my arms wrapped around Dad's neck, being carried into the house and up the stairs to bed, being held in all this joy.

As a child, I would watch all wide-eyed and curious as school halls were transformed into owambe kingdoms that would soon fill with aunties glistening in their high-rise gele and elaborate aso ebi, and uncles shifting in their agbada, occasionally hitching the material over their shoulders as if they were hoisting up trophies. The regal atmosphere that owambe created was the truest of fairy tales, and I imagined how I would look wearing all that majesty. In the future, an older me would stand in my parents' bedroom watching Mum layer my body with a golden fabric that matched her own, her face focused on the intricacies of tying a brown gele with gold accents around my head. This was my crowning glory. And off we would go to yet another party that called us – a child dedication, a wedding anniversary, a joint birthday party for siblings two years apart, a remembrance of someone's legacy, any reason to exalt in community with one another.

In the mix of Nigerian music, food and people in abundance was a particular freedom that introduced me to the sense of celebration at the centre of Nigerian culture. This freedom moved its way from the cultures of owambe and indoor parties and through to the underground dances of my peers. As an adult, dancing became a way to exercise liberation through my body, and when I think back to my early experiences of Nigerian parties, it's easy to see that my love for congregating around music and food and sweaty bodies bouncing off each other like rickety bumper cars was born in D Boss's kitchen, where, perhaps for the very first time, I witnessed how adults moved in the freedom that dancing gave them.

The arrival of Nigerians to the UK, predominantly in the 1970s and 1980s, saw a community that sought to build a home away from home. Some travelled to the UK to study, with plans to return and others came to join family members

" As an adult, dancing became a way to exercise **liberation through my body** " who had already made the move. But this grey country of loneliness didn't understand how to hold the joy of Nigerians on its soil. 'Life in the UK is a boring life. It's a life where people work and die,' D Boss would always say, and many Nigerians who had migrated to the UK felt the same. Their focus became paying bills, providing for their families and sending money back home, and the lack of social spaces made many from our parents' generation even lonelier. Predominantly white schools and workplaces were where our identities went to die. Names that were intended to be affirmations, whispered into the ears of newborns, were shortened to Eurocentric nicknames that British society found easier to digest on job applications and school registers, and Oluwaseun quickly became 'Shaun'. Yet even amid all the difficulties, Nigerians found ways to build ecosystems that maintained their traditions. Ilderton Road in Peckham, south-east London, was the Ibiza strip of hall parties, where the spirit of mogbo-moya made a frequent appearance. 'I heard and I branched' meant you didn't need to be invited to attend – you just needed to know it was happening – and it was more than likely that you would find yourself at the same party as someone you hadn't seen in years, reminiscing all night long. 'I've met a woman that I knew in Nigeria at a party here,' Mum recalls. 'People would meet each other at parties. They might have known each other in Nigeria, both moved to London without knowing and would bump into each other at a party. People find love at parties.' Community halls became pockets of Nigerian culture, and Peckham was nicknamed 'Little Lagos' to capture the growth of Nigerian communities, from the hubbub of the Saturday fish markets to the whistles and clicks of hairdressers signalling you over to their salon chairs.

Beyond the capital, Nigerians spread to other major cities in the UK, bringing their hall parties with them. Igbo House in Liverpool, taken over by the Igbo Community Association, became a central hub that saw many a hall party thrown by a growing community of Nigerians in the city. However, with the onset of gentrification, and consequently the increasing costs of hiring halls, the geographical displacement of a people also translated into the cultural displacement of these traditions. Igbo House became difficult to maintain and fell into dereliction, so Liverpool hall parties skipped between the Social Club and Crawford House in Toxteth, while hall hires came with the caveat of earlier finishing times, meaning people could no longer party into the day. The 'Why not?' aspect of parties soon disappeared, leaving just occasion-based celebrations that were reserved for those vital landmarks in our lives that justified the expenditure.

'In Western parties, there's a lot of chatting. In African parties, there's a lot of dancing,' D Boss laughs with the self-assuredness of a veteran who has seen it all. 'When it comes to parties, trust that it will be colourful.' And I remember the Naija-born soles bouncing off D Boss's living-room floor as if it were a home-sized trampoline. Bodies ducking and double-clapping and hip-rolling to juju music; the aunties loosening their wrappers to allow their waists to twist up against the sound of King Sunny Adé; the uncles swilling brandy out of their cups when the drums of a good fuji track kicked in. Rarely were English songs played at these parties, and if one were to slip through the cracks, Mum says you would hear the people demand, 'Take that off! Put on our music! Let us dance!' – as if the songs were calling them back to the streets of Naija, where entire roads would be closed off to allow for an incoming owambe that would carry on until the people met the sunrise. When the police would come knocking – and they always did – D Boss would simply say, 'This is a neighbourhood gathering!', and all the neighbours who had come would peer through the front door and raise their cups to the boydem, joy dripping down their foreheads, and all the neighbours who had stayed away would hide behind their curtains, snobbery keeping them from a good time.

Having children didn't halt the parties. On the contrary, it created more opportunities to host bigger and better ones. Dedications and birthday celebrations engulfed assembly halls with entertainers, balloons and children's songs – until the parents hijacked the party as the children watched on, half in disbelief, half awe-struck, thinking, *Maybe this is what liberation looked like in a time before us.*

It's easy to forget that our parents have lived many lives before this one, until their memories of their rebellious days capture them in the moment. 'I remember sneaking out to parties with my brother. I'd wrap a nice dress in a bag and leave it near the door, pretend to fall asleep and then sneak out when everyone went to bed!' I sit quietly listening to Aunty Adebanke reminisce about her party days with her daughters – my friend Matilda and her sister Ayo – laughter pouring in between each word. It's a story they've heard before, and they laugh harder each time like it's the first time all over again. 'My dad jumped in the car and came to the party at 2 a.m. with a torchlight, shouting mine and my brother's names. Everyone started disappearing one by one! It was so embarrassing, but I had so much fun.' The three wipe happy tears from their eyes, catching their breath and shaking their heads. 'I enjoy helping my mum get ready for a party,' Matilda says proudly while smiling at her mum. 'I'll do her make-up and help her tie her gele. You forget that she wants to go out and enjoy.' Aunty Adebanke smiles back, letting me know her appreciation of those moments. With the wisdom of an elder, she reminds us of the true meaning of these memories: '"Shake your body and forget your sorrow!" That's what we are preaching. I believe that's how life should be.'

There is a karmic power in the exchange of giving and receiving. The organization of parties is communal: people supply drinks, help to decorate the hall and even stay up until the early hours cooking coolers full of food. If you arrive at the party early, you may very well find yourself immediately appointed as part of the decoration committee and being a child doesn't stop an aunty from putting a spoon in your hand and telling you to come and help serve. 'We don't use event planners, we use our community,' says D Boss. Giving doesn't feel burdensome. It feels like us pouring back into ourselves in the same way rainwater pours back into the land. Despite the structures of Western capitalism, the act of giving and sharing is one that underpins what it means to create community. Parties are a physical manifestation of the sense of jubilation that Nigerians carry, and when we say, 'Naija no dey carry last!', we pull that energy into the spaces we curate for celebration.

According to D Boss, there are three key factors to throwing the best party: good food, good music and space for dancing. 'You cannot have one without the others. If you spend a million pounds on food and your music is bad, they will forget about your food. If you hire the best musicians in the world and have no food, it will kill the party. If you have the music and you have the food and there is no space for them to dance, people will say, "Iru party nonsense wo leyi?!"

Dancing is so symbolic. It is the live wire of any party. People dance to show appreciation.' At any Nigerian party, you can find a huddle of aunties clapping and singing along with the drums of the live band, hailing our names, our foreheads delicately adorned with dollars, feeling like little gods. The culture of spraying money is an affirmation of an abundant life – in the same way Nigerian names are affirmations – and anyone who injects joy into the party could be sprayed.

Live bands act as energy conductors who transform empty dance floors into grounds that surge with the stomping of rhythmic feet. Watching people flock to the middle of the hall the instant Ebenezer Obey, General Ayinola Kollington or Sir Shina Peters tune drops feels like watching the stars populate the sky. 'Playing at hall parties was fun,' reminisces Nigerian drummer Feyisara over a Zoom call as he recalls the heat of the hall party. 'I always had a smile on my face. People would spray me. It was very much about bringing joy to people's faces through music. We would be playing for five or six hours non-stop sometimes.' After all, what is a party without music? 'The music is your cement for the hall party. The food is your block. People attending are the foundation of the house.'

The cultural and geographical displacement of Black joy has never stopped Black communities. We move towards joy by building homes in the community we create with each other. But, with the ageing of the generation of Nigerians who previously upheld these cultural traditions, the hall party is a shadow of itself, trapped in sepia-stained memories. Youth worker Ebinehita Iyere grew up in Peckham in a Delta-Edo household. Thinking about the culture of Nigerian hall parties and Westernization, she states: 'The celebrating for celebration's sake has turned into the materialistic celebration of life. Did we Westernize African parties once we had a choice of whether to go or not? While we were saying no and trying to grow up, did we actually Westernize this without even knowing?'

The stories of British rave culture often don't fully encompass the ways in which Black people in Britain reimagined cultural parties beyond mainstream music genres. When thinking about the evolution of British rave culture between D Boss's generation, my generation, and the generation not far behind me, I recall my very first dance . . .

Aged fourteen, I would wave goodbye to my old self at the front door as a new version of me stepped out into the streets of south London, and each lamp post I passed bathed me in golden light. I had told my parents I was sleeping over at my best friend's house (which, strictly speaking, wasn't a complete lie). The 249 would take Ebony, Zaynah and me straight from Tooting to Clapham Common, moving with the growing anticipation of three teenage girls smothered in

Charlie body spray and excitement. I didn't know what to expect, but I knew that when the dance floor called, I would be ready. Venturing into the back roads of Clapham, we'd bump into a girl in the same year as us at school. Looking us up and down, she would say, '*You're* coming? Rah . . . you lot are bright!', a proud smirk at the corners of her mouth telling us this was the place we would truly meet ourselves for the first time. Here, if only for a few moments, we would be free.

The dance, the function, the link-up, the rave, the shoobs – there were many names dedicated to the release practised on these sticky makeshift dance floors. And when I stepped into the dance, my spirit would be transported back to D Boss's kitchen, watching the adults free themselves and thinking that our outlets aren't too dissimilar. Here, I would begin to understand that on the other side of generational trauma Nigerian parties birthed a generational joy.

As my generation mourns the loss of hall parties, a new era of celebration has begun. Every Friday and Saturday night, the gangan drum calls a crowd of Nigerians to Homerton, where restaurant Eko hosts live bands and serves dodo and efo riro with a side order of faaji. 'Faaji means ultimate enjoyment!' says British–Nigerian chef Yinka Odukoya, who carries on these traditions through Faaji Sundays. 'It's a community that brings people together.' Once a month, Faaji

Sundays opens its doors to the masses, welcoming them in with the pulse of batà drums. Twisting the modern 'boozy brunch' format, Faaji Sundays combines a Westernized weekend event with roots in traditional Nigerian owambe, and Nigerian artists such as Mista Ologo and Wizkid have attended to experience the faaji richness. 'I really want the next generation to appreciate and educate themselves about their culture,' Yinka continues. 'Through Faaji Sundays, I was able to learn about the breadth of tribes and languages just within Nigeria. Educating ourselves about our culture and where we come from is integral. There is so much in our fashion, our clothing, our food, our music. Let it not just be for the good times.'

In the evolution of Black British party culture, we British-born Nigerians have never strayed too far from our owambe origins. The parallels are easy to find. The calls to attention cutting across the music used once to be the slow enunciation of the number plate of whoever's car was blocking the entrance of the hall party but are now the DJ's announcement of a missing phone or provisional licence. The aunties taking off their geles after packing away the party are now the girls switching their heels for trainers at the end of a dance. These emblems of joy continue to trickle down our family trees, planting fresh seeds and reinventing spaces for our bodies to shapeshift into the new dawn. So, when the moon makes space for the sun, which kisses the back of your neck as you hobble home like you own the pavements, you'll ask yourself: whose joy brought you here, and where will you take it next?

FIND YOUR OWN JOY

Put on something that makes you feel royal or your traditional clothing.

"Ask yourself: whose joy brought you here, and where will you take it next?**"**

Keys to the Kingdom
On releasing representation

Haaniyah Angus

WRITER & CULTURAL CRITIC

From as far back as I can recall, film has been a huge part of my life. I adore the intricate world-building, the use of colour and cinematography, and I'm in awe of how someone's small idea can come to life on-screen.

For a long time, I didn't think I would be able to create film myself, but in late 2017 I watched *Lady Bird* and my life changed. Set in Sacramento, California, in 2002, it centres on the relationship between high-schooler Christine 'Lady Bird' McPherson and her mother, Marion, an overworked nurse. Through this coming-of-age film, written and directed by Greta Gerwig, I felt seen in a way I had never been before. Yes, it was about a white American girl, but her experiences were similar to mine. Her complex relationship with her mother resembled mine to a frightening extent, and the pressure on Christine to make something of her life and escape her home town resonated with me. *Lady Bird*'s impact on me influenced my choice to study film at university, something I never believed I would be able to do. I wanted to create my own *Lady Bird* and write stories so young Black girls could feel the same complicated joy I felt when watching a film that moved me.

As well as deciding to create positive representation in my own work, I continued to look for other films that made me feel seen. One, in particular, stood out. *Rocks* (2019) follows a teenage girl, Olushola ('Rocks'), who finds herself taking care of her younger brother after their mother abandons them.

The film is a heartfelt love letter not only to London but to the young Black girls of the city. Even from small moments in the trailer, you can tell how much care and compassion has been placed into its creation. At one point, we see something that is rarely depicted within British films: Olushola's best friend, Sumaya, dresses her up in traditional Somali wear, and Sumaya's mother and aunt compliment her on how she looks. It is a minuscule moment, but while watching it I found myself crying. Not of sadness, but of surprise and joy. There I had seen, for the first time, a true version of myself on-screen.

While I was proud that this representation existed, the internalized film critic in me began to question what representation in film and TV actually means for the Black British community most of the time. You see, there has always been this 'otherization' that occurs for non-white people in British media: we are outcasts only used to fill diversity quotas without genuine support behind any creatives and their visions. This is proven when you look at the 2021 diversity report by Diamond, which captures diversity data for the UK television industry, and see that contributions of 'BAME' writers have had a steady drop from 9.1% in 2018–19 to 6.5% in 2019–20. As a Black film-maker and screenwriter myself, I am saddened to see this occurring, but I would be lying if I said I was shocked.

The othering of Black talent is best explained by bell hooks in her 1992 essay 'Eating the Other: Desire and Resistance':

'The commodification of Otherness has been so successful because it is offered as a new delight, more intense, more satisfying than normal ways of doing and feeling. Within commodity culture, ethnicity becomes spice, seasoning that can liven up the dull dish that is mainstream white culture.' I view her words within the framework of stories being told by those who have no link to the culture at hand. White writers wield their whiteness without taking the time to ponder a single question: am I the right person for this job?'

When I think back to my younger self, a Somali–Jamaican girl who grew up between Saudi Arabia and the UK, there clearly wasn't a chance for me to witness an accurate depiction of myself on-screen. But, at the very least, I had my parents, whose tastes founded my love for cinema and my passion for writing untold stories. In fact, it was my mother's love of Bollywood, stemming from her childhood in Somalia, that had me watching films such as *Kuch Kuch Hota Hai* (1998) and marvelling at the over-the-top dance sequences, the hopelessly romantic plotlines and the glorious 1990s fashions. Meanwhile, my father would have me watch Hong Kong action cinema such as *Drunken Master* (1978). It was here I saw how you could make films without a huge production budget and still rival any Hollywood blockbuster.

Growing up, I held these films from South and East Asia in such high regard. They were masterfully crafted and at the pinnacle of their respective genres – some of the best-written dramas of the twentieth century. I don't believe that a lot of Western cinema can even hold a candle to the way these films make the audience feel, the way they create gripping action scenes, lovelorn romance and riotous dance sequences. I appreciated Bollywood dramas in particular; the sometimes corny action moments and overtly dramatic storylines were such a change of pace from the ever-serious Hollywood rom-com wave of the 2000s.

My background in film is certainly not white or whitewashed, and I am wholly thankful for these inspirations. But for a long time I was angry that I could only rely on non-Black people of colour for a stepping stone into cinema that wasn't shrouded in whiteness. Why were my Blackness and my cultural stories not enough?

I did not know then what I know now: that representation is not a virtue in itself. That perhaps the existence of stories about Somalis in British media need not occur if the voice behind them is clearly distanced from the community. Instead, to find true joy in representation, we should hire those who have a direct link to the stories. There is not only a sense of authenticity that comes with that, but it also allows more Black creatives to enter the industry. Somalis like me have lived in the UK since as early as 1914 and we've become a fundamental part of this country's culture, but this does not mean that

Somali representation on-screen is common. With over one hundred thousand of us, it's clear that there's an abundance of Somali talent waiting to be discovered.

I myself have written several short films, pilots and full-length screenplays centring on Somali characters, from romance to horror, comedy to coming-of-age. One story tells the tale of a young girl finding her first love during the summer before university; another, a story where two friends decide to take the plunge to avoid their parents' disapproval. The same goes for several of my fellow Somali creatives who have written scripts I believe to be more worthy film nominations than those we applaud at the moment. I want to witness moments in film like the tenderness of Somali mothers and aunts putting henna on your hands before Eid day, or historical dramas that expand on the mass migration of Somalis in the 1990s and the communities they have built here.

During my time as a film-maker and screenwriter, I've received my fair share of knockbacks. On the first day of my screenwriting class for my media and film studies degree, I pitched a story, 'Al'akhawat', about two online friends who accidentally discover that they share a father. Not only does this story expand on experiences that several of my Somali friends relate to or have heard of, but it also puts Somali women centre stage in a story where a man has attempted to take away their autonomy. This was inspired by true-life events of mine as well as the mosalsalats (Arab soap operas) I watched as a child with my mother. Their gripping drama and the twists and turns were just another part of what made me want to write for film and television. The response from my screenwriting professor was that my story reminded him of a 'bad soap opera'. This was not the case for a white girl who pitched an updated version of *Green Book* (the 2018 white-saviour film that swept the award season with its 'touching' story of a Black musician with a racist white driver).

At that moment, in front of my professor, the 'otherness' was felt. Blackness in one white-saviour film was groundbreaking, but the Blackness in a Muslim teen drama was melodramatic. That experience dampened my hope of ever having stories like mine seen on-screen, and for a while afterwards I was stuck in a quasi-permanent writer's block, unable to write anything for fear that it would not translate to those I would have to pitch to. I was also furious that I wouldn't have the chance to tell a story from my own cultural background, but for some reason Sally from Lincolnshire would have more authority.

Like most Black women in film and TV, I eventually took matters into my own hands, and alongside my other projects I'm currently developing this story myself. I'm well aware that if I were to do this with a mainstream production company, the elements of my story would be changed, or I would be told that I should *euphoria*-ize my teenage characters for the sake of drama. So I want full control of my work. Even if it doesn't pan out, I'll know that the work is authentically my own. When I look at Issa Rae and her *Awkward Black Girl* web series and how it has been spun into *Insecure* on HBO, it makes me hopeful that one day my own work will find its place. Even so, I know that I cannot solely depend on an industry that does not hire women like me to write stories such as mine. As Audre Lorde stated in her essay 'The Master's Tools Will Never Dismantle the Master's House': 'Those of us who stand outside the circle of this society's definition of acceptable women; those of us who have been forged in the crucibles of difference – those of us who are poor, who are lesbians, who are Black, who are older – know that survival is not an academic skill.'

Representation does matter, but we must make sure that the keys to the kingdom are held by those who aren't the 'acceptable women', otherwise we will be left behind. I imagine a world wherein film-makers like myself can find funding with ease, opening us up as a culture to so many unheard stories of Black joy. Thinking of my own inspirations, such as the 2000s Disney Channel show *That's So Raven*, I'm able to identify the type of media I want to exist. Stories of Black teenage girls living their lives, coming of age, finding love, experiencing hardships that directly link to misogynoir. Not only that but

"The future I want for British film-makers like myself is for us to be in control of our own narratives. I want a young Black girl to see herself represented not only as an on-screen presence but also as a director, writer and producer**"**

I want us to have science-fiction films with Black women as wildly smart scientists, I want more romantic comedies where the leads get to have their own *10 Things I Hate About You* (1999) moments of romantic dedication, and I want creativity not to be hindered by producers assuming audiences just won't get certain stories.

The future I want for British film-makers like myself is for us to be in control of our own narratives. I want a young Black girl to see herself represented not only as an on-screen presence but also as a director, writer and producer.

I believe the way in which we can accomplish this is to have more funding allocated to young creatives; many of us will tell you first-hand how hard it is to afford even basic things such as a camera or a microphone. This can be accomplished through community-led efforts like mutual aid funds, and through pressuring companies and organizations such as the British Film Institute, Film4 Productions and the British Academy of Film and Television Arts (BAFTA) to expand their frankly unreasonable conditions for scholarships, funding and placement plans. As a working-class student myself, I believed I would be able to use these schemes for my own film-making, only to find out I was not eligible because I was in higher education. It's an unfair requirement that tells students from disadvantaged backgrounds that they must choose between their education or their passion. And my passion is so bright.

When I look outside British cinema to films that came out in the same time frame as Rocks, there are others that have set a new standard. *Dhalinyaro* (2019) and *Atlantics* (2019) are both set in Africa – Djibouti and Senegal, respectively – and both have Black women at the helm: Lula Ali Ismaïl (*Dhalinyaro*) and the inimitable Mati Diop (*Atlantics*). While these two films differ vastly in terms of plot, with *Dhalinyaro* focusing on the last year of high school for a group of teenage girls and *Atlantics* narrating the story of a young girl who loses her boyfriend at sea, what they offer is a peek into what it could be like if Black women were consistently given the space to create films about their own girlhoods outside the white gaze.

People such as Barry Jenkins, Regina King, Issa Rae, Nijla Mu'min, Steve McQueen and Michaela Coel also make me believe that this is possible. As writers, directors, producers and stars of incredible films and TV shows, they are living proof that we can create our own stories.

Most of all, they remind me that the future we want can exist – we just have to write it.

FIND YOUR OWN JOY

Write a short story or script that reflects the representation you'd like to see on TV and in film.

"The future we want can exist – we just have to write it "

What Home Tastes Like

How my mum fell in love with souse

Theophina Gabriel

POET, WRITER, ARTIST &
EDITOR-IN-CHIEF OF ONYX MAGAZINE

Illustration by Chioma Ince

'The secret,' my mother says, her eyes grinning at the creases, 'is ketchup.'

*

A little Black girl, not a day over six, observes a flash of silver arching across a hot afternoon sky in Carriacou. The cutlass, a long, sharp blade curved at the tip, is steadied in the hand of an uncle before being skilfully swung down. It's Christmas time, and the pig that has been reared all year for eating is carefully butchered and drained in preparation for the Caribbean festive season. In the pressing heat of the backyard, the girl watches, transfixed, as the meat is sectioned into different cuts, the tripe removed and handed over to her grandmother and mother in the kitchen. Nothing here is wasted. Later that evening, she enjoys the salty taste of her Christmas ham while perched outside with the other children. They are all dotted around, draped on stones and steps in the dusky heat, the sound of soca drifting from inside the house where the adults are.

'Toofi, come.' The little Black girl hears her grandmother, Dada, call her nickname from inside. She leaves her stone, placing her plate down carefully before walking up the steps and into the house. The elders are all sitting around the table, and her eyes drift hungrily over the various bowls before settling on her grandmother's face and the silver spoon being cradled to her mouth.

'This is for you,' Dada says, smiling as she spoons some broth and trotters between the little Black girl's lips. Souse is a delicacy, one usually saved for the elders, but Toofi has always been her grandmother's secret favourite. As she catches her first little taste of pig's feet – the kick of the scotch bonnet, the thyme, the garlic, the infusion of spices – her eyes widen with the magical realization of falling in love with her favourite dish for the first time. She looks down at the bowl of golden-brown broth and smiles.

*

I lean back in my bed in the darkness, flicking between Uber Eats, Just Eat and Deliveroo. I am teasingly, if not lovingly, known as the Takeaway Queen among my circle of friends. It's just so convenient having a range of hot-food options at your fingertips and deliverable in under ten minutes. My mum disagrees with me, shaking her head disapprovingly every time she hears yet another knock at our front door. One day when she comes into my room, clutching a familiar brown paper bag, I decide to ask her what her favourite dish is and her eyes light up brighter than my phone screen.

'Souse,' she grins.

'Pig's feet?' I ask in mock horror as I sit up slightly, trying not to judge. 'Isn't that like the jelly stuff?' I pull a face.

'The gelatine? Oh yes.' She laughs. 'That's the best part!'

If I'm being honest, the whole concept of pig's trotters

grossed me out. When moving down the line for food at the function with my trusty polystyrene plate, I'd always gratefully welcome the rice and peas, the heavenly curry goat, a delicious square of mac and cheese, the crispy fried chicken; I'd beg and plead for *just one more* slice of fried plantain, nod and nod some more while the gravy was being poured. But when Auntie pointed to the side dish of trotters or pig's tail? Myth. I remember shaking my head quickly, fingers outstretched to receive my full plate safely back into my hands.

'Why do you like it?' I ask my mother curiously.

A spec of guilt settles when she replies. 'I guess it's a dying culture. Maybe your generation wouldn't understand . . .'

*

After that first taste at Christmas, the little Black girl watches the backyard with a hawklike gaze. She waits patiently on the stone steps, but no matter how long she watches, there is no uncle and no carefully swung machete. She asks Dada about pig's feet while she combs coconut oil through the old woman's long silvery hair one night. Dada smiles, telling her she must wait until next Christmastime. Here, everything moves slowly and in time with the demands of the seasons alone. Only on special occasions – a feast for an elder, when someone returns home from abroad, or Christmas – are the animals slaughtered. Being the main sources of their livelihood, the animals are carefully reared throughout the year and saved for celebrations; and, unluckily for her, Christmas has just passed. Dada tells her that cow foot tastes similar, and her heart leaps when her grandmother informs her that someone down the road is thinking of slaughtering their cow. She warns her granddaughter not to get her hopes up – her chances of tasting it are slim because there are, after all, only four feet. Souse is a delicacy in fierce demand and it's not usually reserved for children. The girl secretly hopes anyway despite her grandmother's warning, and when the cow is finally slaughtered, the feet are snapped up quicker than she can ask Dada to request one. The disappointment of going without so much as a taste bitters her mouth.

*

'Once in a blue moon,' my mum recounts wistfully, 'and when you got it, oh, it was like a treat!'

I sit up fully, trying to imagine what the wicked injustice of only being allowed plantain once a year would feel like.

'How does it taste?'

My mum shakes her head. 'Unlike any other dish you've tasted. It's not made out of meat, but the way it's cooked is incredible.'

She describes the way the gelatine is drawn away from the bone with intense boiling until it softens, how steady your hand must be as you place the scotch bonnet into the pot whole with bomb-disposal-like precision; it is only ever one burst away from ruining the entire dish with a hellish heat. As the water boils, the pepper shrinks slowly while the feet absorb its spice. The whole process takes hours, the jelly gradually absorbing the flavours and setting against the bone until it fattens under the soft skin. Her joy, however, lies in the way the salt used to preserve souse can find its way right into the centre of bone.

'So where did souse come from?'

My mum pauses, and as her hand cradles her chin I take a moment to think too. I think about the way food is a map of our past, and how we can lose our sense of place with the dishes we forget to remember.

'I'm not sure where souse originates from,' she finally replies, her brow furrowing, 'but I'm sure it came from slavery times; when we were given the parts that the slave master didn't want.'

'I'm going to look into it,' I say, reaching over for my laptop and typing my curiosity into a fresh tab.

*

Souse was a dish created on the fringes of need, in a desperate battle against hunger. Originating in England and European countries during the Middle Ages, it was known as a cold cut: a type of food that could be preserved for long periods of time by salting or pickling in vinegar. Cookbooks dating back to the seventeenth century instruct readers to even bury food in

" I think about the way food is a map of our past, and how we can lose our sense of place with the dishes we forget to remember **"**

the ground for preservation during the long winters. British recipes typically depict modest seasoning – a bay leaf and onion would usually be suggested alongside some mustard – and the dish would be served with a slice of bread.

Once relative wealth had been acquired through colonial violence, souse fell out of favour with the gentry and was picked up by working-class peasants and servants. British colonizers brought the knowledge of their dishes with them to the Caribbean islands, and souse, now a dish associated with the lower-working classes, went from being something that was eaten by white servants to a meal that was passed on to Black African slaves. Food was used as a weapon of control, and the enslaved were regularly starved or given the undesirable offcuts of meat. However, unlike their British predecessors who would season the dish with little more than salt and a bit of pepper, Black African slaves in the Caribbean ensured that the pig's feet were infused with enough spices to make up for the lack of meat. They would then be boiled for hours until they gave up every inch of what could be eaten.

Souse was a meal of choice for runaway slaves, as its ability to be preserved for a long time was critical during their long journeys of rebellion. Centuries later, food in the Caribbean is still tinged with survival and preparation. The slow processes of gathering and preserving are carried out with the ultimate goal of creating dishes that are well flavoured and filled with sustenance, summed up with the well-known phrase of 'belly-full'.

This well-seasoned dish was eventually passed down as a delicacy, usually served in its own sauce as a side dish. The history of Caribbean souse is one of reversing undesirability and turning preservation into pleasure. It is the radical persistence of the rich flavours of Black joy, even from the margins of deprivation and survival.

*

The little Black girl stares at the elders' full bowls of souse with envy every Christmas. Despite being grateful for the little tastes she's afforded by Dada, she still craves a full bowl of her own. She won't get one until she sets foot in the UK as a teenager, her mother bringing her and her sisters over during the Windrush era. It's a fitting full circle for a dish that originated in England.

It's a Saturday morning in the late 1970s, the air is crisp with cold and it's not a minute past nine, but already Shepherd's Bush is bustling with Black Brits doing their weekend shop for their various meats and wares. Her mother doesn't have to tell her to stay close: one silent look shot through a glaring eye is enough to convey the level of discipline required. She presses closely to her mother's side as they enter the market.

The market moves with the pace of a torrent; a current

of purposeful bodies sweep anything without a direction away with it. Among the hive of the busy meat and fish stalls, the teenager and her mother gather all the pieces of chicken, pork and yam that are harder to find back at their local Asian shop, Rocky's. She can barely contain her joy when their haul includes four whole pig's trotters. An uncle with a flat cap and curly white beard chops the feet into parts. The cuts are smaller than the ones made from the machete's blade back home, but she is still giddy as her mother lets her accept the cerulean plastic bag. She grips it religiously all the way back to Slough in the back of the car alongside her sisters.

When they get home, her mother shows her how to prepare souse in the same way her mother showed her. She watches eagerly and in anticipation as they wash the feet with lemon and season the meat with peppers. When she places the scotch bonnet carefully into the pot, it conjures up the warmth of Dada's smile at Christmas – and the flavours that have tantalized her ever since – until her heart aches and her mouth waters.

*

'So, Dada told Grandma to put ketchup in her souse?' I ask. My curiosity has admittedly piqued in the time it has taken my mum to explain, and a notebook has materialized in my efforts to capture a bit of my cultural history.

Chioma Ince

'No,' my mum quickly corrects me, 'your grandma, my mum, was the one who told me to put ketchup in souse. We discovered ketchup in England, and Dada never set foot over here.'

I put my notebook down. 'So where did you make souse for the first time?'

'Over there,' my mum says, pointing to our kitchen.

'Really?'

'Really.' My mum nods. 'Your grandma said the ketchup settles everything just so, and it does. It adds a lovely base alongside all of the spices.'

I laugh with the realization that this is a Black British twist on a Caribbean remake of an English dish as my mum eyes me curiously.

My laughter soon evaporates when I try to pin down the exact recipe. 'I never measure really,' my mum says as she shrugs her shoulders, noting hazy measurements that shift between 'a teaspoon' and 'a tablespoon'.

I chew on the end of my pen and put it down. 'OK then, can we make some together?'

'You – ' my mother raises an eyebrow – 'in the kitchen?'

'Yes, me!' I shoot back at her, my eyes widening in mock offence.

*

'My favourite part is the colours,' my mum says as she beckons me over to look.

I nod in agreement as I peek over her shoulder. 'It looks like a painting, all the reds and greens and yellows.'

Although I'm enjoying this rare moment of being in the kitchen, I can't help but think of all the things probably bubbling over on my to-do list. My mum picks up on the impatience in my feet, as mothers do.

'We didn't like the kitchen either, you know,' she says, raising her brows and pushing her mouth up. 'All yuh have it too easy. We didn't want to be in the kitchen, but we didn't have a choice. Six thirty every morning to get started on the cooking and cleaning.'

I think guiltily about the way convenience has divorced me from my culture. I make an effort to still my feet and take in the smell of the seasoning instead. I think about the distance between me and back home, noting it in geographic and cultural miles, thinking about all of the methods of preparing food that were necessary. My mother tells me stories of okra necklaces strung up in the kitchen and fish dried out on the roof in the sun. Of slow dishes and preservation, food cooked and prepared to the rhythm of dry seasons. I glance at my phone and the flash of brightly coloured apps on display before turning it off. Even if I don't necessarily like these dishes, I'm determined not to let the cultural knowledge of them, even pig's feet, die out with me. I savour my mum's smile as we move around the kitchen.

As my hand carefully places the scotch bonnet into the pot whole, I pause as I imagine the hands of my mum and grandma and Dada doing the same. Growing up in a country with supermarkets that sell skinned chicken eight different ways may mean that I will never learn how to kill and prep a whole one from scratch like they did, but as I deliver the scotch bonnet safely into the pot I feel closer to them than ever.

'OK, so what's next?' I ask.

'I like to put the pot in the oven with some foil over it, because it's better at trapping the water underneath,' my mum says, handing me an open can of butter beans to pour in. 'If you put it on the stovetop without a cover, you have to keep replacing the water as it boils, but in the oven underneath the foil the water has nowhere to go.'

She nods in approval as I place the tinfoil over the mouth of the pot, and when I close the oven the rush of heat on my face lingers like the memory of stepping into Grenada for the first time.

*

A wonderfully heavy smell of broth fills the kitchen as the souse boils in the oven. After five hours, the woman gives a nod – the souse is finally ready.

She sits down at the table, watching as her daughter dishes up, pouring the feet and the sauce into two bowls.

Her daughter is still wary about the texture, but as she spoons the golden-brown liquid around the feet her determination sinks in. The notebook lies face down on the living-room sofa, forsaken mid-recipe. For generations, their ancestors have seasoned by eye and by taste, remembering the way things are made, unwritten.

Her daughter joins her, setting down their two bowls of souse on the table. The little Black girl, now a mother, looks from her bowl to her daughter's watchful face. She smiles at her before eagerly delving into her bowl of souse, her hums and murmurs of enjoyment spilling through a tissue, which she dabs to the side of her mouth. Her mind revels in the teenage memories of her first bowl within these very same four walls. Through the corner of her eye, she catches her daughter's nervous glances.

'Go for it,' she instructs, grinning daringly. 'Bite around the bone.'

Her daughter lifts the spoon to her mouth, analysing the gelatine and the white butter beans. As she takes her first mouthful and the kick of the scotch bonnet catches against the back of her throat, she finally understands. She makes a note of the the heavily seasoned sauce, taking in the unique flavour of this Black British history now unfolding on her tongue. As her teeth work at the gelatine to break it down, she understands the toughness of preservation, the resilience of survival swallowed into a warmth that fills her belly. The texture is quite unlike anything she's ever tasted before and she's not sure whether she likes it, but she understands. She takes another spoonful to pay tribute to the generations of patience, the stolen souse holding a runaway slave's hunger at bay for a while longer, the years of trapped heat and endless boiling. Still undecided, she takes one last bite, and when her teeth suddenly graze the centre of the feet she discovers the surprise of her mother's joy in the perseverance of the salt, all the way to the bone.

FIND YOUR OWN JOY

Ask a friend or family member what their favourite cultural dish is. Tell them yours and then plan a date to eat each dish together.

More Than a Monolith

Understanding my mixed-race identity

Ruby Fatimilehin

WRITER & EDITOR

To my eternal embarrassment, at birthday parties, wedding receptions, Christmas dinners and family gatherings, my mother will reminisce to those congregated about a day out at the zoo when I was a toddler. Without any encouragement from me, she'll chronicle the hours we spent trawling around pens filled with hirsute goats, funky-smelling bat caves and shimmering aquatic tanks until we finally arrived at the enclosure of my favourite animal: the flamingos. According to my mother, I stood at the railing with ice cream smeared across my face, bouncing up and down on my tiptoes to peer into the enclosure. After a moment of deep contemplation, a smile lit up my face as I exclaimed, beaming through baby teeth, that the flamingos were 'pink, like Daddy!', amusing my mother, a Black Nigerian woman, to no end. Proud of my discovery, I staunchly refused to accept that pink people were in fact called 'white' because 'if flamingos are pink, so are they!'

Hearing this story for the hundredth time, I can often be found rolling my eyes and blushing faintly, but the anecdote never fails to receive a few giggles or, if aided by several glasses of wine, slapped knees and hearty laughter. Playfully highlighting the constructed nature of race, the story reveals that the terminology we use at times does not match reality, often to humorous consequence.

Growing up, I spent countless school holidays gallivanting

about, causing mischief with my mixed-race siblings and cousins. We constructed intricate pillow forts, suspending blankets between creaking bunk beds with 'GIRLS RULE BOYS DROOL' and 'SCHOOL SUCKZ' scratched into their frames. Endlessly resourceful, we'd drag damp towels off washing lines and hijack cushions, scooped up from under the bottom of a bemused uncle or auntie, part of the constant stream of visiting Nigerian and English family members. T-shirts became castle walls and skirts were fashioned into the sails of pirate ships, vexing our parents when some snagged seam inevitably unravelled. We used anything we could get our hands on to assemble technicoloured caves in which younger siblings were invariably 'NOT ALLOWED'. Once, we even managed to stretch the sheets of our fort so taut that for a few moments we could crawl across the fabric, suspended mid-air like spiders on a web, before the structure came crashing down. We fell to the ground, cocooned in cotton, belly-laughing with aching limbs.

Each summer, my cousin Josh and I would take turns visiting each other for a week, spending our time between London and Manchester. When in London, we would drag Josh's go-kart to the park and lug it to the very top of the hill before speeding back down the concrete, screaming with laughter, our faces shining like conkers in the sweltering heat. As soon as our parents turned their backs, we jumped on the bus down to Kensal Green high street. I was appalled that the other transport users didn't say thank you to the bus driver when exiting the bus, something that had been drummed into me back up North. We bought magnifying glasses from the corner shop, which we used to burn dandelion fluff and the pages of old schoolbooks, starting a little fire in the park. After being scolded by parents and park-keepers alike, our magnifying glasses duly confiscated, we wasted no time rushing on to our next scheme. Fancying ourselves little potion masters, we would concoct 'herb water' out of plants found in the garden and attempt to tout the swamp-coloured beverage to anyone unfortunate enough to pass Josh's house. The height of our trade was when a generous uncle offered us a fiver for a cup, delighting Josh and me to the extent that we didn't notice him discreetly pour the liquid down the sink.

During my stay, I would wrinkle my nose at the astringent tap water and defend shortened vowels, arguing that 'the word "fast" describes something fast – it should be said *fast* not *faaarst*!' But I loved London; loved walking around Notting Hill Carnival in the sizzling summer heat, devoid of Mancunian drizzle; loved buying clear plastic bags filled with sticks of sugar cane; loved lying on the grass ('not *graaarss*!') devouring the tough white flesh, sucking out syrup from coarse fibres.

After a week or so, Josh and I would take the train back

up north to Manchester's red-brick houses, charcoal-coloured skies, and canals laden with half-submerged shopping trolleys breaking the water's surface like breaching whales, alluding to some midnight mischief the night before. (When studying in Leeds a decade later, I stumbled across a maquette of a proposed statue by Antony Gormley, the sculptor behind the Angel of the North, when wandering around Leeds Art Gallery. Enthralled by the 120-foot red-brick man who would have towered over the city, I lamented that it had never come to fruition, so much did it encapsulate my love of the urban sublime of the industrial north.)

As we entered Manchester, the train would slow, winding across graffiti-covered bridges, past scrap heaps whose twisted metal sparkled in the sun, the light refracted, penetrating deep into murky canals below. We would cruise past thistles and bindweed, past ragwort which I knew would be peppered with black-and-yellow cinnabar caterpillars, past the perfumed purple buddleia whose pollen the train's final gasps would propel far into the air. I was deeply touched by the scenes that flickered past, by the foxglove and cornflower that bloomed through the rust, resiliently enduring in the industrial landscape.

Josh was a massive Nirvana fan and quickly indoctrinated me. We took frequent trips down the high street to Kingbee Records, where I spent my pocket money on 50p CDs with scuffed cases and faded sleeve notes. During one train journey I remember Josh, aged nine, and me, ten, nattering to each other about the 27 Club, detailing the tragic deaths of Kurt Cobain, Jimi Hendrix and other minor deities. The man sitting across from us commented on our conversation, saying we had 'very mature music taste' for our ages. Oh, the approval! It was mainly Josh's influence, but I grinned to myself all the same.

Josh and I would spend the week meandering along the Mersey, watching *Fresh Prince of Bel-Air* reruns and entertaining every scheme that entered our young brains, joyfully revelling in our uninhibited self-expression. I truly cherished our time spent enjoying the freedom of childhood, but eventually term would begin and Josh would return to London.

At the start of term I would make my way to school, meandering through the park, collecting acorns and playing with the other kids. We'd link daisy chains and pull up fistfuls of cow parsley to throw at one another, rolling around in the grass until our hair looked like sucked mango stones. At playtime, we gathered under sycamore trees, cradling our Tamagotchi toys and discussing the pros and cons of chewing thumb holes in the sleeves of our school jumpers (pros: truly the height of fashion; cons: facing the wrath of parents, who 'aren't made of money, you know!').

One day, a girl giddily approached me and some of the girls from my class, ladders running down her tights, and claimed that the boys had confided in her who they fancied. She was known for telling tall tales and I was instantly dubious about the quality of the information. Hadn't she just last month announced she was going to invite the whole year to a huge party that, of course, never materialized? She was certainly not a reliable narrator, but I knew her information would reveal who she assumed the boys liked, so I hung around to listen.

She began the matchmaking process, first listing the most popular, blonde-haired girls then carefully selecting blue-eyed boys of a similar social rank to pair together. Her declarations were met with protests and flustered giggles as the eyes of those gathered darted to search their friends' faces for any glimmer of truth. As she progressed through her list, one of my friends asked, 'Who likes Ruby?', to which the girl answered in a matter-of-fact tone, 'No one.' How embarrassing! I didn't fancy any of the boys, nor did I care if they liked me, but the knowledge that she believed none of them would be interested still stung. There was no malicious intent; it was simply a foregone conclusion, out of her hands, giving me my first inkling that, to white society, my appearance and identity were undesirable.

Unlike Josh, who was more self-assured than me and firmly

identified as 'mixed race not Black', I began to consider it a losing battle to fight against a society that uniformly labelled me Black. Originating during slavery, the one-drop rule permeates the fabric of Western society, maintaining that an individual with one distant Black ancestor is 'tainted' by Black blood for generations to come and forever severed from white identity. When a mixed-race person with one Black parent is racialized, they are often placed in the same racial category as their Black parent. This conception of race trickled down to my childhood years, which I spent trying to decide which box to tick when filling out ethnicity sections of forms with no mixed-race option. White friends and teachers would tell me: 'You're Black, so just tick Black.'

Although I often had no choice in being racialized as Black, I also began to willingly embrace this identity due to the promised comfort of belonging. As the only mixed-race student with a Black mum and white dad in my year at high school, the allure of belonging to a larger racial category greatly appealed, so I attempted to forge a racial identity by conforming to behaviours and attitudes assigned 'Black' by wider society.

Nirvana was abandoned, replaced with Frank Ocean and Earl Sweatshirt, and I found a sense of community with the small number of Black girls in my year. We spent lunchtimes sitting in the dining hall playfully bickering over the superiority of Nigerian or Ghanaian jollof rice and arguing about the pronunciation of '*plantaain* not *plantin*!' We rolled our eyes and kissed our teeth when white classmates on a hockey tour in South Africa filled our Instagram feeds with photos of themselves posing beside orphaned Black children. I remember a group of us, having grown up attending Pentecostal churches, singing renditions of songs from *The Prince of Egypt* and shouting across the corridor 'God is good!' to be answered 'All the time!', much to the confusion of our classmates.

But any attempt to conform to a societal conception of Blackness is inevitably doomed to failure. Blackness is viewed by British society as a monolith of behaviours and stereotypes, so much so that all Black people are expected to act and feel the same. Any Black person who deviates from this homogeneous idea of Blackness faces being labelled a racial outsider, not 'truly' Black, often by Black and white people alike. During my stint with vegetarianism, one Nigerian classmate stated, 'Ruby's not really Nigerian, she's vegetarian!', revealing the two identities to be mutually exclusive, much to my surprise! At the same time, white friends would say, '[insert white person's name] is Blacker than you,' based on their preconceived notions of Black characteristics, namely coolness and a lack of intelligence.

Although exacerbated by my mixed-race identity, all

Black people face an expectation that they must conform to societal stereotypes of Blackness or else have their racial identity questioned. But stereotypes alone are incapable of encapsulating the whole of a human being, their tastes and interests, likes and dislikes. No matter how I curated my hobbies and behaviours in pursuit of a 'truly' Black racial identity, I would never be able to match up, so uncompromising is the confining stereotype of Blackness and so quick the rejection of any behaviours deemed un-Black. In my early teen years, I hadn't yet come to realize this – or perhaps I subconsciously chose to brush any niggling doubts away, so desperate was I to be embraced within a wider racial community.

I felt I'd been denied any claim to British identity by white society and assigned the label of Black other, and so, like countless other members of the diaspora, my homeland became a mythical place with the potential to venerate my Black formulation of identity. Following in the footsteps of writers such as Audre Lorde, who, in *Zami*, imaginatively transformed Grenada into a place that embraced all aspects of her identity, I imbued Nigeria with the power to explain my place in the world.

When my parents announced to me, aged fifteen, that we would be travelling to Nigeria for a family holiday, I was ecstatic. As children, my brother, sister and I had briefly shared a bedroom and each night my mother would sit on the red-cushioned chair between our beds and read to us from her collection of Yoruba fairy tales. We would listen, spellbound by stories of magic gourds and foolish kings, and of Oluronbi, who attempted to trick the talking Iroko tree. The two silver bracelets she wore would chime as she gesticulated earnestly, cradling the pages with hands that shone like polished oak. These nightly tales ignited my love of stories while contributing to my perception of Nigeria as a mythical place, sculpted by my mother's tongue.

Disembarking from the plane in Murtala Muhammed airport in Lagos, I was startled to find everything so tangible. For a place that had previously only existed to me in stories, the humidity which pressed itself into my lungs and the bustling people adorned in vivid clothing seemed larger than life. It was the rainy season and vegetation pushed its way through every crack. Every patch of dirt erupted with mango and pawpaw trees, the rich soil giving life to hibiscus blooms, which glowed ember-red through smoke rising from roadside barbecues grilling suya. Unlike Manchester's perpetual drizzle, the rain in Lagos poured out of the sky without warning, drenching anyone unfortunate enough to be caught outside, before ceasing as abruptly as it had begun. The ferocious sun quickly sucked up any remaining moisture, often leaving me to wonder if the downpour had been some strange dream.

As I sat squished in the back of a car on the way to visit a distant relative, a feeling of unease began to spread through my body. I had expected this mythical land to venerate my attempts to conform to a Black racial identity, but instead I was confronted with the realization that Black identity in Nigeria was very different to the one I had attempted to construct.

Back in England, surrounded by Black friends and family who often can't speak their mother tongue and have never visited their homelands, some Black British people find a sense of solidarity through opposition to a racist white society, unifying irrespective of their countries of origin. But in Nigeria, a political Black identity created in opposition to whiteness was ill-suited as the vast majority of the population were Black Nigerians. My mother told me that growing up in Nigeria, she had never thought of herself as Black in the same way she did once she moved to England, where she was suddenly a minority. In Nigeria, I realized that my conceptions of what it meant to be Black were completely British, the very thing I'd been trying to escape!

I mulled over these different formulations of Blackness for the rest of the holiday, turning contrasting ideas over in my mind while watching my mother barter for pink coral necklaces at the market, eating huge plates of pounded yam and egusi in relatives' homes, and traversing suspended walkways through the rainforest at Lekki Conservation Centre, pink

" I perceived the power in welcoming difference across Blackness and viewing variation **as strength rather than weakness "**

crabs scuttling into sodden holes between mangrove roots far below.

Towards the end of our trip, we went to visit Nike Art Gallery, a beautiful building with a dazzling exterior, white as a cowrie shell bleached by the sun. On the day of our visit, Mama Nike, the owner, was entertaining a group of businessmen who were interested in purchasing artwork. A flawless hostess, she guided the men around the gallery, which had Adinkra symbols embossed on its walls like raised marks of scarification. She breezed around the place in her traditional iro and buba, with navy Crocs peeping out from under the hem of her outfit, her shaved head crowned in a giant indigo-coloured gele that spread a metre across. In her striking clothes, she effortlessly combined Nigerian traditions with her own personal flair. Observing the comfort and ease with which she mixed different cultural modes was the catalyst that allowed me to finally realize I didn't have to conform to any one conception of Blackness but could instead embrace the multiplicity found across Black identities. I perceived the power in welcoming difference across Blackness and viewing variation as strength rather than weakness.

During my time at university, this anti-monolithic conception of Black racial identity flourished. Offering refuge from the overwhelmingly white space of higher education, Black Feminist Society embraced the various textures of Blackness, rejecting racial conformity and creating a community in which we can truly be ourselves. Some of my favourite memories from university are of the potlucks where we would sit together cross-legged on the carpet, laughing and chatting while cradling plates of food cooked by society members: smoky jollof rice, rich peanut stew and sweet plantain the colour of amber. Together we vented our frustration at the injustices we faced, offered support to one another and passed down advice to first-year students.

When building relationships and tackling the difficulties and dilemmas that are an unavoidable part of life, I take inspiration from the way I used to play with my cousins when I was little. I remember the fun and mischief that permeated my childhood and use this sense of adventure as a tool to approach life's challenges, exploring and delighting in the various forms and expressions of Blackness, and using childlike creativity to create a space for togetherness across difference.

FIND YOUR OWN JOY

Gather together all the blankets and cushions from your sofa and make a pillow fort! Experience the joy found in playing like a child.

"Exploring and delighting in the various forms and expressions of Blackness, and using child-like creativity to create a space for **togetherness across difference**"

Entering the Scene

Finding a community of love

Jason Okundaye

AUTHOR & JOURNALIST

SATURDAY 29 AUGUST 2020

Are you going or nah?
Cause I really don't know lol

I really am undecided

It just doesn't feel right to be
ayying on insta story right now...

If I go it'll be last minute.

Within a few hours of these WhatsApp exchanges, my best friend, Jere Agbaje, and I were indeed 'ayying' on our Instagram stories, in attendance of a Black gay housewarming in Streatham Hill, hosted by our mutual friend Lyra. Mind you, this sea change from indifference to merrymaking wasn't one of those standard emotional rituals that precede late-night motives, where you ebb and flow between hesitation, nonchalance and enthusiasm. When we'd begun messaging at around 7 p.m. that day, we were miserable.

That morning, Black people across the world had woken up to yet another doom klaxon – that Chadwick Boseman had died following a private battle with colon cancer. Not to reduce the actor's legacy to a singular role, but it felt manifestly cruel that in a year that had so far been defined by the endless theatre of Black death – families left bereaved by police brutality; Black people losing their lives to coronavirus after being viewed as a non-priority to enter ICUs in medical triage; Black expectant mothers dying suddenly, with their maternity shoots leaving us with a kind of techno-hauntology – Black Panther himself was gone.

I'd spent the day in bed, doomscrolling on Twitter, reading tributes, watching old videos of American children reacting to the news of a school trip to watch *Black Panther*, and laying digital flowers for a man who had come to embody Black diasporic unity. Naturally, I didn't feel like partying – I dismissed making space for joy in these circumstances as a frivolity. It just didn't feel appropriate. But what encouraged me to carry my load to Streatham Hill was that I hadn't been on the scene in so long. I hadn't seen my community: the Black gays, lesbians, bisexuals, queers and transgender people of London. By 'the scene', I mean the ever-shifting locations where we show face, congregate, gossip, brunch and whine.

The coronavirus pandemic had locked off everything. No Black queer raves, no house parties, no brunches, no Black Pride. 'Black Pride being postponed has really hit me. Do you know how much the community looks forward to Black Pride? We talk about it year round, I was even already thinking about outfits,' I tweeted on 23 March, knowing that 'postponement' didn't mean an autumn or winter celebration; it meant the event wouldn't be happening at all in 2020. And Black Pride is Christmas Day for the community – I'd give anything to be there in Haggerston Park, like I was in 2019, showing off my newly muscled physique in tight shorts and an Adidas crop top, hoping that *this* would be the Pride to give me that blockbuster romantic moment where I finally meet my husband. So I knew that even if it felt heavy to lift myself out of this bed and this grief, I wouldn't forgive myself if, for all my public lamentations, I didn't swim across channels to reach the first Black gay social event since lockdown restrictions had been semi-relieved.

Over the spring lockdown, Jere and I had reminisced about our early debuts on the scene. Among our broader Black queer social group, we're the 'baby gays': kids of the Blair era among children of Thatcher and Major. So we felt especially mournful for the enjoyment we were missing, because those early years on the scene, before the full weight of employment and bills came crushing down on us in adulthood, were meant to be about pleasure-seeking and daring each other to dive off the speaker at the next rave. I remembered some of those lawless nights we enjoyed.

One of our fondest memories is Queer Bruk, an LGBTQIA+ dancehall night, which was being hosted at Vogue Fabrics Dalston – an airless sweatbox where lack of ventilation didn't prevent us from delivering and receiving the wickedest whines. Onlookers who witnessed us emerge from the underground club, with steam rising from our foreheads and our clothes crumpled like foil, may have thought we had escaped an oven and not a basement. But the freedom and catharsis of the gay rave, of moving with freedom and without fear of judgement and harm, produces those delightful rhapsodies that transcend you from the heat and the sweat and the dark so you could as well be dancing on clouds as in a dungeon; all that matters is that there are no mental chains or restraints. These queer spaces are so joyful for me because it is world-making ambition and imagination that bring them into existence. These are spaces that render culture a religion and a sanctuary where one can escape that which perils us.

It was the world-making ambitions of Queer Bruk's founder and host, Akeil Onwukwe-Adamson, that allowed the space to blossom from humble beginnings in a small dungeon-like venue to sound systems, regular features on the radio and a more cabaret affair in larger dimensions, with vogue battles and catwalks. I remember seeing Akeil at that Queer Bruk in summer, emanating maximum drama by swanning around the venue in a pink tulle dress which remained poofy and elegant, refusing to be weighed down by the soaking humidity. We love Akeil on the scene because

" These queer spaces are so joyful for me because it is world-making and imagination that brings them into existence **"**

he's such a main character, so of course he wore the Big Pink Dress of the moment. Think Angela Bassett's fuchsia Reem Acra gown at the Academy Awards in 2019, or Tracee Ellis Ross's hot-pink Valentino cloud dress at the 2018 Emmys, or Rihanna's princess-pink, empire-waisted, tiered, tulle Giambattista Valli frock at the Grammys in 2015.

Akeil makes clear to me that the joy of this night is as much about celebrating himself as celebrating the rest of us Black queers. 'Queer Bruk was always about *me*, primarily,' he waxes sentimental over voice notes and, I think, glasses of prosecco. 'It was always about the music that I grew up on, and I just wanted to create a space which reimagined my life in Brighton. Which brought my queer world and my Black world together. And Queer Bruk is also about the music. It's always been about African and Caribbean music, Afrobeats, dancehall, soca, and bringing those together in a queer world.'

The building of entire worlds within dance and music spaces for the safe and joyful expression of identity has a long history in Black Britain. Queer Bruk is but one of the latest expressions in a long genealogy of club nights. Speaking to *Boyz* magazine for Black History Month in 2016, legend of the scene Calvin Dawkins, otherwise known as DJ Biggy C, emphasized the importance of memory work as a community, to remember the spaces that we've built and lost over the years.

As a long-time resident DJ of the Black LGBTQIA+ night Bootylicious, which has been the nucleus of the Black queer scene since it premiered in the early 2000s, Biggy C commented to *Boyz*: 'There has always been a vibrant and exciting club scene for Black LGBT people in London. However, it's existed outside of the mainstream and as a result we have created our own.' But he also acknowledged that these nights often die out due to financial insecurity or dwindling public interest, meaning that the variety of the scene has in fact regressed over the years. 'Twenty years ago there was more choice. We had spaces like Kudos, Fruit Machine, The Vox, Queer Nation, Low Down, Biessence and Caribana. And you could guarantee that there'd be at least two house parties every weekend.' And indeed, much of our experience of the scene in terms of nightclubs is chasing these nights around London, as the lack of a fixed and permanent venue specifically for Black LGBTQIA+ people (unlike, say, the superclub G-A-Y Heaven) means that near enough any district of inner London could be the new mecca to which the Black gays complete their pilgrimage. Bootylicious itself moved from Club Colosseum in Vauxhall to Electric in Brixton, and then back to Vauxhall again in Union Club. I remember regularly attending the club night Pxssy Palace with Jere at Mick's Garage in Hackney and, after its increasing popularity meant it needed a larger venue, at The Garage in Islington.

Despite the lifting of restrictions that summer, nightlife was not graced with a return, and so the scene has relied on the housewarmings, parties and gatherings like the one hosted by Lyra. Frankly, Black queer house parties have provided me with a kind of joy and intimate magic that is unmatched by other aspects of the scene. These parties taking place on housing estates with predominantly Black British populations remind me that the ends are a diverse home for Black queers, even if popular media refuse to see us. These house parties have unhurried warmth. They're where myths and legends of the scene are created and brought to a head. They're where you truly get to know, and know about, people without the double-cheek-kiss-and-move-on speed and pretensions of more public spaces. My friend Derrien Layton, who debuted on the scene half a decade before I did, describes the unique magic of the house party to me:

> 'My first experience of Black gay nightlife in general was a house party in 2011. I remember me and my friend Kwame went up to Bedford. And it was exciting for me because obviously the scene is so small here, we gossip amongst each other, there are a lot of legends and a lot of tales. So the house party was a space where I could finally put a face to these legends and these

" It kind of serves as a reminder that there's magic in community...

it will always be a safe space "

tales. And it kind of doubles up as a reminder, especially for people who are just coming into their sexuality and just starting to make other Black gay friends, that it's not just you in this world as a Black gay man. It kind of serves as a reminder that there's magic in community. And that's even if everybody doesn't get on in that space, because that does tend to happen, as there can be arguments and disagreements and the like. But you know those disagreements and tensions aren't because of your sexuality, so in that sense, regardless of your tensions, it will always be a safe space.'

It's this element of myth and legend, of storytelling, narrative, names, faces and characters, that I describe as the 'quiet joy' of the scene. Don't get me wrong, the house party of 29 August had so many loudly joyful moments. Singing in chorus to Nicki Minaj's unreleased 'New Body' verse, City Girls' 'Act Up' and Vybz Kartel's 'Virginity', as queer Black women around me grinded on each other (no boy-on-boy action as I was, God knows why, the only gay boy at this house party – Lyra, I'm still mad about this!), was blissful and reminded me of just how much I missed dancing and DJs. I adore how much we loudly gas each other up on the scene, complimenting a good beat, taking pictures, handing out gold medals for the smoothest waist movement. Umairah and Sameera, our South Asian friends within the broader scene of queers of colour, fed us with the most deliciously spiced chicken wings, which we were all dying to know the recipe for. And I can't not let my audience know that the Black queer ladies told me that I, without competition, 'have the best ass in south London'.

This said, I felt most content and joyful in those quiet moments of reflection when I absorbed my surroundings and realized just how much the architecture of the Black queer scene made possible for me. I grew up with a very early and very doomed sense of my sexuality, and I couldn't have ever imagined being in a community with an entire pantheon of people like me. And while I'm now a very confident Black gay man, there was once a boy who thought he existed alone in this world. In those quiet moments you can speak, think and feel with real clarity.

The storytelling that takes place in the breakout rooms when you take a breather from the dancing is always my favourite aspect of house parties. Lingering in a breakout room is often unfairly described as antisocial, but it's here that you crack jokes, catch up on gossip, let people know about your plans and your dreams and how much you love them. I remember Jere and I popping upstairs and chatting for what felt like hours with Lyra and her girlfriend, Maya, talking about whether we'd assimilate into the institution of marriage, speculating on who will have the first Black queer wedding (streets are saying it's Rose), gushing about Jere's and Maya's careers, about Lyra's upcoming projects and photography, about my ambitions to write and one day produce documentaries and dramas.

It's in these bubbles of love, when you find those brief moments of time to appreciate the blessing of being in community, of having a 'scene' at all, that joy surfaces in the chaos as a cooling, calming, ontological affirmation of life and the value of togetherness. The joyful chaos of parties and club nights is a kind of ecstasy, but it is incomplete without the smoking areas and bedrooms where we bond and get to know each other. Equally, the more perilous chaos of an anti-Black world, one which often forces us to surrender into retreat and isolation, doomscrolling on our phones, being force-fed the bodies of the dead, anxious about the next terror, can be quelled by the resolute determination to continue dancing, and laughing, and dreaming, and sharing stories. Jere lucidly recalls her emotions from that night at Lyra's – she's clear that the scene had brought her joy as comfort in a time that had been indexed by social isolation and collective mourning.

'Attending Lyra's house party was absolutely surreal.

It felt so special to exist as my entire self, and to just feel so vibrant and present in that moment.' These words from Jere reminded me of the sanctity of those spaces where you can be 'your entire self' for those Black LGBTQIA+ people who don't have the luxury of self-expression at home with their biological families. As so many of us have existed or continue to exist within these constraints, parties like Lyra's give something to believe in. 'It just felt like a morning stretch on a warm summer's day,' Jere continues, 'with the sun shining and all the warm happy things that we tend to think of coming together at once. It was building bonds, seeing people that you've built bonds with online, because of our shared community, actually seeing them in the present and what they look and feel and sound like.

'And it sounds ridiculous, but I wasn't expecting much as well,' she says, remembering our mutual hesitation at attending. 'I remember being on the train and trying to grin my way into putting on a facade of being present and sociable, and immediately, when I did get there, that just washed away. I think it made me realize just how important these physical spaces are and how much we take them for granted, because lockdown took them entirely away.' Joy for me is in the quiet of this realization. It is in the knowing that there is a community of love, of celebration, not mere tolerance and acceptance, in which your interior self is your exterior self. Joy is in the peace and safety of community and togetherness. I can't stop thinking about how wonderful the scene is, and how much happier my life is for having found it. Right now, I miss my Black gays and my gays of colour. Jere, Isi, Cleveland, Lyra, Maya, Derrien, Tosin, Martha, Nana, Rose, Twiggy, Umairah, Sameera, Paul, Ismail, Tanya, Marc, Tochi, Che, Nadia, Zareen, Timi. I miss seeing them at the nightclubs, the dinners, the lunches, the brunches, the birthdays, the parties, the coffee catch-ups. They are my scene, and they are my joy.

FIND YOUR OWN JOY

Find yourself an elder person, in the Black gay scene or Black Britain at large, and speak with them. Share stories with each other and exchange notes about your experiences of partying, loving, and finding community today and 'back in their day'.

" [Joy] is in the knowing that there is a community of love, of celebration, not mere tolerance and acceptance, **in which your interior self is your exterior self** "

It's Like Candy

The bittersweet salve of social dancing

Vanessa Kisuule

WRITER & PERFORMER

Illustration by Tomekah George

Press the 'on' switch to this memory.

A tiny bedroom, dodgy carpet, walls thin enough to hear your neighbours' thoughts. Scuffed but loyal speaker working overtime on a bedside table. The song playing is barely a week old, but all of you sing along like the lyrics were etched under your tongues from birth. You've been waiting all week for tonight and it's finally arrived, dressed in indigo and sparkles. In front of the mirror, Kaya moves her waist in lazy circles, her body unheeding of the hindrance of bones. Girl can dance and she knows it, always rocking crop tops so her waist beads glint under the lights. Jade's more chill with it, gun fingers lifted as she sends air bullets to the ceiling. Jordan bops his big head up and down. When the beat kicks in, his face crumples like someone's just farted. And Luke, well, Luke can't dance at all, and all of you rinse him for it. He's Bambi after two blunts, chasing after the beat like it owes him a fiver. All over the world, variations of this scene unfold on any given evening, with dance as warm-up ritual and main event, the glue that binds us under one beat. This right here is joy, with all its force and fleeting footwork.

I can't write about dancing without writing about Sean Paul. When I was twelve, I bought his album *Dutty Rock* on CD. Stuck in the stifling confines of boarding school, a cluster of us Black girls gathered round to listen. I would often find the disc missing from its jacket, slyly 'borrowed' by one of the gang who hadn't scrimped and saved hard, like *moi*, to get her own copy. On weekends, we'd camp out in the computer room, which was kitted out with massive, wheezing Macintosh desktops. It was there we first saw the 'Gimme the Light' video. Hats slung low and dark skin shimmering, the dancers moved tight to the groove, their steps so incisive that I wasn't sure if they were responding to the music or vice versa. The distinction between glossy pop videos and reality was yet to develop in my fledgling mind. I assumed adult life would be like a Sean Paul video, and I still nurse huge disappointment that it's not.

The choreographer behind the video is Tanisha Scott, a powerhouse dancer of Jamaican heritage who is credited with being the first to bring dancehall movement into mainstream music videos. She was not formally trained but instead honed her skills in recreational centres and clubs, the informal spaces where freestyle dancing blossoms. It's this looseness that gives the video its distinct flavour, the sense that anyone can get up and join in. We quickly learned the difference between their magnificence and our messiness when we tried to copy their moves and looked nowhere near as cool.

Lucky for us, the video for 'Like Glue' featured a dance break dedicated to moves like Row the Boat, Signal the Plane and Gi' Dem a Run, which were easy and fun to do, allowing plenty of room for personal flair. Simplicity is the key ingredient of a good dance trend: instructional lyrics and repetitive movements that are for toddlers, Freedom Pass owners and everyone in between. This formula expands beyond the Caribbean, of course. I have fond memories of UK funky hits in 2009 that sparked some silly but infectious dance trends: K.I.G.'s 'Head, Shoulderz, Kneez and Toez' took a nursery rhyme and updated it for the ravers, while Gracious K gave us the Migraine Skank, which required nothing more than miming the gestures of suffering from a headache. For those who never quite know what to do with their limbs, these communal dances are a low-stakes way to catch a vibe. This is how YMCA gets even the clumsiest of folks into an excited froth – if we can't dance, maybe we can at least spell.

In my teens, Jamaican culture reigned supreme. Reggae, bashment and sound-system parties all boasted universal appeal. On top of this, we were fed an overwhelming glut of African American music that became shorthand for Black music in its entirety. I didn't feel shame around my East African heritage per se – more a buried sense of its irrelevance in popular Black culture. Now, the diasporic influence is broadening as Afrobeats blows up in popularity and with it a stunning array of dances from South Africa (Gwara Gwara), Nigeria (Shaku Shaku), Ghana (Azonto) and many others. The current generation is embracing and embellishing their ancestry, forging a fresh vocabulary of movement boosted by this international renaissance.

Though there's no age limit on dancing, it does lend itself to youth, unsaddled as it is by creaking joints or aching backs. I miss that blissful hinterland of being thirteen, watching and rewatching *Honey* and *You Got Served*, wearing patches into the carpet from practising my heel-toe. Though the prospect of puberty hovered, dancing remained a bonding exercise rooted in play rather than posturing. Sometimes we filmed our efforts on the very basic camera phones that existed at the time. Thank God Snapchat and Instagram didn't exist then; with no pressure to gain likes or shares, we basked in the catharsis of moving for its own sweet and simple sake.

Social media does deserve some dues. It's not only a platform for exposure but also a forum for dancers to claim credit for their ingenuity and influence. TikTok, for example, seems tailor-made for the contagion of dance crazes, and, unsurprisingly, young Black people have been at the helm of this. Atlanta's Jalaiah Harmon was fourteen when a dance she created called the Renegade blew up in early 2020. Sure enough, there came a steady tide of invariably white imitators who did their own versions, gaining followers, fame and even cheques. But thanks to diligent efforts by the dance community, Jalaiah's story was covered in a full profile in the *New York Times*. For all its problems, the internet can help reverse the erasure of Black creators.

Despite how disparately we are scattered, the importance of community demonstrates itself in every part of the diaspora. In Sean Paul's 'Get Busy' video, a hot and heavy party is in full swing in the basement of a family home. A young boy in pyjamas sneaks into the rave, breaking into a spirited dance to the amusement of everyone around him. He is soon hustled back upstairs, where the sensible elders are sat eating and talking. I read this as a subtle love letter to how we occupy space, defying the Western dogma of the nuclear family and retaining the blurry continuum of friendship, relatives and acquaintances. We see this in African gatherings that stretch past their guest lists, in the tiny clubs whose size belies their electric atmosphere. We've been taught to associate modest space with deprivation, but I've felt my happiest in rooms bursting with loud aunties and annoying cousins, broad-shouldered boys and bronze-cheeked girls with braids that move like pendulums as they sway. Give me this over any air-conditioned superclub in Ibiza.

At sixteen I went to my first club. There, I was initiated into the Mack Daddy of Black dances: the Electric Slide. It was my cousin's birthday and the floor was heaving with young Black teenagers from ends. The DJ played 'Candy' by Cameo, and, to my surprise and slight panic, the crowd began to move in unison. *Is this a thing?* I thought, my feet in a petty squabble. *Yep, this is clearly a thing*, I concluded, as the crowd shuffled from left to right and then suddenly forward. For Kent-dwelling Vanessa of 2007, this was an unwelcome ambush, a test of Blackness I'd woefully failed.

Though the Electric Slide was created in 1976 by Richard Silver, the original dance, consisting of twenty-two steps, was adapted into the simpler sequence we know today. The Slide can be danced to any song with a steady beat, but it is forever intertwined with Cameo's 'Candy' due to the classic final scene from the 1999 Black American movie *The Best Man*, where the wedding party breaks into the dance. The Slide is now an unquestioned staple – the song that any self-respecting DJ will drop to get a crowd going. Everyone springs to action when they hear that spiky bass.

Well, everyone apart from 2007 Vanessa.

I was a listless salmon swimming upstream, catching dagger eyes as I trapped someone's foot under mine. But then, through repetition and sheer force of will, muscle memory worked its invisible magic. The sequence's logic unlocked itself and my feet stepped and rose of their own accord. Finally, mind and body aligned and the groove could reign. By this point, it's fair to say I was feeling my oats. In fact, I was the whole damn porridge (sorry). I started adding my own inflections, lifting my leg as I pivoted, dipping my body low as I stepped side to side. There it was: the smug satisfaction of getting it right, that sweet synchronicity of belonging.

Tomekah George

Stripped to their essence, the steps of the Electric Slide aren't dissimilar to those in line dancing or a Scottish ceilidh. What sets the Slide apart is the *way* you step, how the staccato funk of 'Candy' gives the dance its laidback cool. The two-step format is present in not just the Electric Slide but also the Dougie of 2010 and 2004's aptly titled '1, 2 Step' by Ciara. Mining the lineage of these dances is somewhat like opening up a Russian doll: the cakewalk that enslaved Africans would dance on Southern plantations sitting inside the exuberant Charleston of the 1920s sitting inside the intricate footwork of Memphis jookin sitting inside the frenetic bounce of South African house.

Name the dance style and I've probably had a stab at it, from ballet right through to belly dance. As soon as I hit university, I took full advantage of the subsidized dance tuition and became a member of the ballroom and Latin dancing society. Stepping into my first session, I had a bloated sense of confidence that I was swiftly disabused of. While I had a general aptitude for rhythm and performance, I lacked polish and the formal ballet training that ballroom technique is built on. Dancesport also favours conventional beauty, expensive costumes and a lean, disciplined body. Now imagine me: a picky 4C 'fro, G-cup tits and jiggly thighs that loved to do their own choreography independent of the rest of me.

Reader, it was a grade A shambles. I would consistently be cut in the preliminary rounds. The judges' eyes would glide over me and my partner before moving on to couples with nicer costumes, stronger technique, the star quality that eluded me. With no shiny prizes to show for my efforts, what was the point? Staring down the gulf between who I was and who I desperately wanted to be, I questioned if I had the grit it would take to bridge the gap. There were two options: either double down and give up yet more time, money and sanity in the pursuit of perfection, or admit defeat. After two years of competing, I chose the latter. Pants hairsprayed to my arse and itchy lashes dangling like windscreen wipers, I realized that enjoyment was not a price worth paying for excellence. I still think wistfully of what could have been, but comfort comes in knowing I need not possess inordinate talent to appreciate that type of dancing. As a humble witness and admirer, I make my worthy contribution.

The pressure-free sphere of social dancing brought me back into my body. This arena of dance operates like good conversation: through feeling, responding, mirroring. Breakdancing, voguing, dancehall and other vernacular dances from the diaspora are now taught in professional studios across the world to people of all races, an inevitable result of grassroots art rubbing up against the demands of commerce. But these dances are more than the sum of their steps. They are a living, morphing record of who and why we are. Hip-hop dance was informed by the polyrhythmic movements of African dance, and dancers in contemporary Africa are now, in turn, influenced by their US counterparts. We also see the trace of other cultural influences: the martial arts-inspired lines in waacking, the melding of contemporary and ballet technique with West African styles that birthed jazz dance. This is the upside of an interconnected world built on porous exchange, a creative utopia where collaboration usurps ownership and innovation is a higher virtue than categorization.

But in our current system, money and individual prestige trump social cohesion. We waste energy debating who 'owns' a dance step, who can patent it, package it and sell it to the highest bidder. If the forces of white supremacy and capitalism weren't so strong, we wouldn't need to fight so hard for these props. My choice to shout out Tanisha Scott in this essay is a deliberate corrective. I highlight her rather than the many non-Black choreographers making a living teaching and choreographing in a dancehall style. Not all of them are cynical opportunists, but it's telling that some of these teachers enjoy huge popularity while their Black peers languish in relative obscurity. With the finite energy I have, I want to celebrate artists like Scott who have forged successful careers despite the pervasive biases in the commercial dance world.

Now let me address my dance-shy people, because representation matters. The stereotype that all Black people can dance is maintained by folks of all races, including our own. We are not only expected to be good but effortlessly so. We can't be blamed for upholding this flattering assumption, but stereotypes of any ilk are harmful. Young women especially are bombarded with the symbolism of dancing as potent social currency: a means of showing off an attractive body, winning the attention of men and the admiration of other women. Not many insults sting like being dismissed as 'stiff' or 'dancing like a white girl'.

So-called race science made unfounded claims about our innate dispositions, including that we were fundamentally less intelligent than Europeans and biologically built for slavery. We know this to be untrue, but we must also challenge other specious notions around how *all* Black people behave, even when those ideas seem empowering or unifying. We can gather in common purpose without leaning on even lazy mythologies. No, not all Black people have 'natural rhythm' or even dance the same – big up the Nigerian wedding party moshing to System of a Down, and African American Irish dancer Morgan Bullock kicking and shuffling to Megan Thee Stallion. To the awkward shoulder-boppers, head-bangers and shame-faced people furtively YouTubing how to twerk: solidarity. You belong here too.

All joy sits in close parallel to its opposite, and the Black dancer stands under a long shadow of exploitation, too often an avatar of light relief or deep suspicion. Skepta's 2015 single 'Shutdown' addressed the moral panic sparked by him and other grime musicians dancing alongside Kanye West at the BRIT Awards. In a skit halfway through the song, a white woman's nasal vowels quiver with trepidation as she laments the sight of 'a bunch of young men all dressed in black dancing *extremely aggressively* on stage'. Skepta plays her middle-class fear for laughs, but beneath this playful braggadocio is frustration at being a pawn in a fruitless culture war. There's no better visual for this perpetual misunderstanding and disconnect than the offending performance itself: a tangle of Black men on stage wreathed in their glorious, infectious energy while clusters of nonplussed audience members sit rigidly at their champagne-laden tables. The atmosphere curdles with a dissonance this country has yet to reconcile with. Some people will always view us scathingly, especially when we're having too much fun for their liking. It's someone's problem for sure, but not ours.

Where others see threat and deviance, I see gangly kids in hand-me-down tracksuits losing their shit to Lethal Bizzle's 'Pow!', carried on a fizzing wave of childlike chaos.

I see a fluid whine between two strangers, a playful teasing that doesn't necessarily mean they're going home together but rather that the groove dictates the moment – and their bodies are but willing followers. As Audre Lorde told us, erotic energy can infuse everything we do and is wasted when reserved purely for the act of sex itself. Our spontaneity and sensuality are habitually divorced from their context and thus robbed of their beauty. When we focus on self-definition over self-defence, we're free to view our culture on its own nuanced terms.

Dancing, in its purest and most holistic form, is less about doing and more about being. We deserve to just *be*, not as second-class citizens or magical creatures but ordinary humans, wealthy in spirit and worthy of unconditional dignity. Dancing shakes loose the cobwebs of loneliness and banality, returns us to the blissful, brutal fact of our finite lives and fragile bodies. These morsels of freedom that briefly make us feel immortal never last long enough, but there are worse ways to spend a life than chasing them on the wind.

On my deathbed, I'll be greeted by a mystical hybrid of my twelve-, sixteen-, twenty-five- and seventy-year-old self, her eyes closed and arms raised mid-movement. She'll be too lost in music to hear me. I will sigh a contented sigh, go where souls go when breath takes leave of the body. At my wake, the DJ will drop 'Candy'. Everyone will exchange looks, get up from their seats and report for duty. They know exactly what time it is.

FIND YOUR OWN JOY

Put on a song you remember from your schooldays and dance – not to look good but to feel free.

" Dancing, in its
purest and most
holistic form,
is less about
doing and
**more about
being** "

About the Editors

Charlie Brinkhurst-Cuff is an award-winning journalist and the former editor-in-chief of *gal-dem*, a magazine dedicated to people of colour of marginalized genders. She's also edited and authored a book of essays about Windrush called *Mother Country*. When she's not disrupting British media, she can be found baking cakes, eating cakes and playing football.

Timi Sotire is a music and culture journalist who's profiled stars such as Dua Lipa, Bree Runway and Jazmine Sullivan. Outside writing, she works in the editorial team at Apple Music. Her dream interviewee is the Alabama rapper CHIKA, but she'd obviously love to interview One Direction – if they were still together!

About the Contributors

Diane Abbott is Britain's first Black female MP and the longest-serving Black MP. She's the daughter of Jamaican parents who came to the UK as part of the Windrush generation, and she is passionate about the writing of Alice Walker and reggae music. Her favourite food is chicken and rice 'n' peas.
My Black Joy song: 'Sun is Shining' by Bob Marley

Faridah Àbíké-Íyímídé is a fiction writer whose debut novel, *Ace of Spades*, has been described as '*Get Out* meets *Gossip Girl*'. She grew up in Croydon, south London, and is studying English literature at a Scottish university. Her hobbies include collecting quirky mugs and rewatching Disney Channel original movies.
My Black Joy song: 'Schoolin' Life' by Beyoncé

Fopé Ajanaku is a reluctant writer who lives in London and pretends that they're not enamoured with the city. They write about intimacy, identity and sexuality. They also believe the art of good romcoms has been lost to the sands of time (also known as the early 2000s) and this week their favourite romcom is *10 Things I Hate About You*. They don't make them like Patrick Verona any more.

My Black Joy song: 'Is This Love' by Corinne Bailey Rae

Athian Akec is an eighteen-year-old activist, writer and speaker. His main areas of focus are climate change, youth violence and racial inequality. He's written for the *Guardian*, *Independent*, *Huffpost*, *i-D* magazine, *Huck* magazine, *Hunger Mag* and other national newspapers. He's been profiled by *The Times* and *i-D*. Athian has spoken in the House of Commons as a member of the UK Youth Parliament. Athian also sits on the board of a youth charity and commission in Camden focusing on economic renewal following the pandemic, and is a special advisor to a Parliamentary inquiry into the teaching of Black history in British schools.

My Black Joy song: 'Voices' by Dave

Travis Alabanza is about all things theatre, whether it's producing, writing or performing. In 2019, they turned a transphobic attack into *Burgerz*, a one-person play that won an award at the Edinburgh Fringe. Their all-time favourite outfit is a bright blue faux-fur jacket, for special occasions!

My Black Joy song: '1999' by Prince

Haaniyah Angus is an internet culture and film critic who's been published in *Vice* and *Vulture*. She focuses on elements of Stan Culture, online activism and memes in her writing, as well as race, gender and class. Haaniyah is also a director and screenwriter, with her short film *Misplaced* set to come out later this year.

My Black Joy song: 'See You Again' by Tyler the Creator

Rukiat Ashawe is an award-winning sex educator, writer and content creator who uses her platform to speak about various topics surrounding sex and relationships, society and culture. Through her work she challenges stigmas, advocates for better sex education and triggers thought-provoking conversations. Her interest in philosophy stems from her current studies in sociology.

My Black Joy song: 'Come Together' by The Internet

Bukky Bakray is the youngest winner of the BAFTA Rising Star Award. She is finding her way through the industry, describing her dream career as a 'slow burner'. She loves discovering music, film, a number of different art forums and life, which all inform absolutely everything she does.

My Black Joy song: 'Another Life' by D'Angelo

Richie Brave hosts *1Xtra Talks* on BBC Radio 1Xtra. He is the son of a Guyanese father and Anglo-Indian mother. His creative endeavours have largely been influenced by nearly two decades of community-based work. His true passion aside from connecting to others is music and its ability to carry listeners on endless journeys to the past, present and future.

My Black Joy song: 'Gabriel' by Roy Davis Jr

Munya Chawawa is a British–Zimbabwean comedian, writer and broadcaster who's known for his satirical online sketches. Across his various social media platforms, he has amassed over 1.5 million followers including the likes of Trevor Noah, John Boyega, Stormzy and the elderly couple in the downstairs flat. When he isn't risking his own deportation with politically charged TikToks, he can be found practising dance moves in the mirror, in the event that JLS ever need a stand-in at their reunion tour.

My Black Joy song: 'Universe' by Ty Dolla $ign

Ruby Fatimilehin recently completed an English literature degree at the University of Leeds. She is also a writer and a poet who was runner-up for the Mairtín Crawford Poetry award at the Belfast Book Festival 2020. She is British–Nigerian and her favourite food is plantain.

My Black Joy song: 'I Wanna Be Your Lover' by Prince

Theophina Gabriel is an award-winning poet, writer and artist from Slough. When not working on creative projects, she can be found heading up *Onyx Magazine*, an independent publication that champions Black creatives. In her essay she aims to explore and preserve the history of joy that belongs to older generations because the history of Black joy is as important as its present and future.

My Black Joy song: 'Sir Duke' by Stevie Wonder

Lauryn Green is a university student with a love for screenwriting and storytelling. She's currently in her first year and plans to work on her creative portfolio to bring her stories to the screen. Her favourite hobby oscillates between sleeping and (badly) playing piano.

My Black Joy song: 'Crazy Classic Life' by Janelle Monáe

Ife Grillo is an award-winning poet and writer, and a former world debate champion. Growing up in Hackney, he got involved in local campaigning which led to him becoming Vice-Chair of the British Youth Council and the first-ever Young Trustee for the NSPCC. He's taught young people all over the world about the power of debating, community and storytelling.

My Black Joy song: 'Superheroes' by Stormzy

Isaac James is a multi-award-winning lawyer by day and a lyricist, composer and writer by night. His writing centres around Caribbean languages and cultures, Blackness, sexuality and disability. His songs are heartfelt, evoking strong emotions that all humans can relate to. He co-founded the award-winning Black Men in Law Network in 2018, which helps the current and next generation of Black boys enter the legal profession. He's a Black pansexual, neurodivergent Caribbean man – who lives for all iterations of Carnival around the world.

My Black Joy song: 'Jab Forever' by Skinny Banton

Chanté Joseph is a writer, content creator and host of Channel 4's *How Not To Be Racist* and *The Face* magazine's 'My Public Me' podcast. She has written for the *Guardian*, *Vogue* and *Vice*, and her favourite publication *gal-dem*. Her first book, *A Quick Ting On: The Black British Power Movement*, is due out in 2022 and when she's not working the keyboard she's working the pole as a pole fitness enthusiast.

My Black Joy song: 'Liquorice' by Azealia Banks

Vanessa Kisuule is a poet and writer living in Bristol. She's currently writing a collection of essays about her childhood obsession with Michael Jackson.

My Black Joy song: 'Soul Makossa' by Manu Dibango

Henrie Kwushue is the host of KISS FM's *Wake Up* weekend show and the 'Who We Be Talk' podcast on Spotify. She also runs her own production company, HTK Productions, and has made two shows, *Is Your Area Changing*, a docuseries about gentrification, and *Untold Stories*, a web series about personal stories around different topics. Alongside her presenting, Henrie can be found DJing her favourite Afrobeat, soca and dancehall tunes aka 'music for bum shakers' at festivals and events across the UK.

My Black Joy song: 'Jumpin' Jumpin'' by Destiny's Child

Tobi Kyeremateng is a writer and producer born and raised in south London. She founded the Black Ticket Project, which distributes tickets for live cultural experiences to working-class young Black people and has written for the likes of *gal-dem* and the *Independent*. The only thing she loves more than parties is plantain.

My Black Joy song: 'Jaiye Jaiye' by Wizkid (feat. Femi Kuti)

Mikai McDermott is a multi-disciplinary creative who has fostered partnerships with a variety of beauty, fashion and lifestyle brands. Having completed a master's degree specializing in Caribbean gender history, Mikai uses her online platforms to create and share her research on the continent. Five years of creating with a collective audience of over 100,000 has enabled Mikai to become a unique voice within an underground culture that embraces the complex relationship between beauty, fashion and Black history.

My Black Joy song: 'Essence' by Wizkid

Jason Okundaye is a journalist who writes about culture and politics for the *Guardian*, *GQ* and *Dazed*. His first book, about the history of gay Black men in his native south London, will be published in 2023.

My Black Joy song: 'Fantastic Voyage' by Lakeside

Tope Olufemi is a beatmaker, writer, and politics and sociology student at the University of Warwick. At the time of writing this piece, Tope was in the process of growing locs.

My Black Joy song: 'Let Go' by Demae (feat. Joe Armon-Jones)

Melz Owusu is the founder of the Free Black University, an organization committed to radically imagining the possibilities of education around the world. They are a former member of Black Lives Matter UK, and a decolonial activist with a focus on trans lives and education. Melz is doing a PhD in sociology at the University of Cambridge. They grew up in south London, but feel most at peace by the ocean and surrounded by trees back home in Ghana.

My Black Joy song: 'Blessings on Blessings' by Oshun

Leigh-Anne Pinnock is a member of Little Mix, one of Britain's biggest-selling girl bands. She's also the founder of swimwear line In 'A' Seashell and will make her acting debut in December 2021. Leigh-Anne has a tattoo that reads 'believe' on the back of her neck. She got the tattoo when she was eighteen years old and it was inspired by her belief in making her dreams a reality.

My Black Joy song: 'Millionaire' by Andre 3000 and Kelis

Mayowa Quadri is the brand and editorial officer for football platform Versus. He lives and breathes the beautiful game and has been a pundit for CNN and the BBC alongside being a content contributor for *Copa 90* and various online outlets. Mayowa spends the majority of his time preaching about how sport can be a tool for societal change. Despite having the opportunity to speak to footballers past and present through podcasts and gaining a reputation for being a conversationalist, nothing replaces the feeling of scoring three goals at seven-a-side and bragging about it in a group chat. He may talk the talk, but he can still walk the walk.

My Black Joy song: 'Sue Me' by Wale

Lavinya Stennett is a writer, and founder and CEO of the Black Curriculum. Graduating with a first-class degree from SOAS in 2019, she has continued writing on Caribbean and

Black histories. Lavinya was on the *Sunday Times* 50 Women of the Year list and was awarded Trailblazer of the Year by *Hello Magazine*, as well as featuring in *Vogue*, *gal-dem* and *GQ* for her work.

My Black Joy song: 'Finish Line' by Chance the Rapper

Sophia Tassew is a plus-sized content creator who encourages people to be their authentic selves, utilizing her platform to start conversations that inspire changed behaviour and attitudes. She is also an art director turned small business owner and designer for her handmade earring line called Khula, which draws on her East and South African heritage. She has converted her passions for community and culture into a book about jewellery within the Black diaspora, and has also curated multiple sell-out exhibitions that reflect on different subcultures that exist in and around London. Her style icon is Lizzo, and what she'd most like to achieve is a comfortable life for her family and herself.

My Black Joy song: 'Joy' by Leven Kali

About the Illustrators

Jovilee Burton is a digital artist based in central London. Her illustrations are inspired by a love of nature, colour and patterns. She loves: to create illustrations that evoke a sense of the body, mind and soul; fun, loving characters; exploring a range of female characters for her audience with uplifting messages around positivity, health and wellbeing. Jovilee's passion is listening to music and reading books as these are things that fuel her creativity.

My Black Joy song: 'I Can' by Chronixx

Tomekah George is an illustrator based in Sheffield, UK. She's inspired by her current surroundings and early Caribbean upbringing, which was full of colour, laughter, jokes and music.

My Black Joy song: 'I'm a Big Deal' by Christopher Martin

Emma Hall is a designer from Cambridge living in Lisbon, Portugal. Her work is at times graphical and almost always digital; she attributes this to her formative years studying architecture at Newcastle University. Her mother is Mozambican and her father is English.

My Black Joy song: 'To Be Young, Gifted and Black' by Aretha Franklin

Chioma Ince is a British–African and Caribbean illustrator and workshop facilitator whose work explores themes of politics, identity and narrative. She is passionate about representation, social change and championing inclusivity within the arts.

My Black Joy song: 'Africa' by D'Angelo

Olivia Twist is an illustrator, arts facilitator and lecturer from east London. The key threads that can be found in her work are place and the mundane. Footwear is her thing; the passion started when she was about six or seven when she got her first pair of TNs.

My Black Joy song: 'Toast' by Koffee